THE POWER OF
Teacher
Talk

The Power of Teacher Talk

Promoting Equity and Retention Through Student Interactions

Deborah Bieler

Foreword by Valerie Kinloch

TEACHERS COLLEGE PRESS

TEACHERS COLLEGE | COLUMBIA UNIVERSITY

NEW YORK AND LONDON

Published by Teachers College Press, 1234 Amsterdam Avenue, New York, NY 10027

The author wishes to express gratitude to those granting use of the following:
Photographs on the front and back covers are used with permission from the photographer, Kristen Boylan (http://kristenboylan.com).

Portions of Chapter 6 appeared in "The Critical Centrality of Social Justice in English Education" by Deborah Bieler and Les Burns in *Innovations in Pre-Service English Language Arts Teacher Education* (Heidi Hallman, Ed.). This material is used by permission of Emerald Publishing.

U2 lyrics from "Zooropa" in the Epilogue appear with the permission of Hal Leonard, LLC.

Library of Congress Cataloging-in-Publication Data is available at loc.gov

Names: Bieler, Deborah, author.
Title: The power of teacher talk : promoting equity and retention through student interactions / Deborah Bieler ; Foreword by Valerie Kinloch.
Description: New York, NY : Teachers College Press, [2019] | Includes bibliographical references and index.
Identifiers: LCCN 2018032846| ISBN 9780807759578 (acid-free paper) | ISBN 9780807777343 (ebook)
Subjects: LCSH: Teacher-student relationships. | Teacher turnover—Prevention. | Dropouts—Prevention. | Educational equalization. | Motivation in education.
Classification: LCC LB1033 .B5155 2019 | DDC 371.102/3—dc23
LC record available at https://lccn.loc.gov/2018032846

ISBN 978-0-8077-5957-8 (paper)
ISBN 978-0-8077-7734-3 (ebook)

Printed on acid-free paper
Manufactured in the United States of America

26 25 24 23 22 21 20 19   8 7 6 5 4 3 2 1

This book is dedicated to
Jordan Michele and Kimberly Mae

And to those for whom you're named
—especially Lucille Mae Hillegass and Michele Evans Smith—

—beautiful, spirit-filled, loving, inspiring women, all—

May you always act justly, love mercy, walk humbly (Micah 6:8),
and follow your dreams, even and especially when they seem difficult.

And to all of the teachers and students
who create beauty as they interact in their classrooms every day.

Contents

Foreword

"But how do you stop a child from falling when you're falling faster?"

Bieler, 2011, p. 4

So, how do you stop, prevent, and/or interrupt the fall of a child when you are fully aware that you are already falling yourself? What do you do? What can you do? How do you come to terms with the daunting reality of seeing someone else falling—a child, at that—as you are already falling in ways that feel unstoppable and that make you feel powerless? What . . . Do . . . You . . . Do? And how do you find the support you need to do what you need to do?

These are some of the difficult, alarming, and heart-wrenching questions I grappled with as I read Deborah Bieler's book, *The Power of Teacher Talk: Promoting Equity and Retention Through Student Interactions*. In fact, these are some of the very same questions that have jarred me and brought me to tears many nights. Maybe it is the painful reality of knowing and seeing that a child is falling and that you cannot immediately stop the fall. Maybe you do not even know there's a fall that's coming and that you should work at stopping it before it even happens. Maybe it is that you are trying to prevent the fall at the same time that you are falling or in the process of falling, and falling rather quickly. Or, maybe it is the devastating realization that you were not taught (or shown) how to stop the fall as you fell through the teacher education program that prepared you to work with our children and young adults inside schools and communities. For as many "maybes" I can list about not being able to stop a child from falling, there are just as many "what ifs."

What if every teacher were fully supported to creatively, inventively, and innovatively engage with children and families in learning environments committed to nurturing their soul, spirit, and their whole being? What if each and every teacher received this same type of engagement and was supported to interact with students by relying on discourses of, and practices in, love, care, and compassion? What if Damian, a high school student of color, in one of the classes Bieler observed, were treated by his White English teacher with respect and viewed as knowledge-filled as opposed to knowledge-less? What if classrooms, specifically, and schools, generally, were sites of imaginative, creative, hands-on, and critical learning and not sites of racial microaggressions? What if children and teachers were fully and lovingly supported to fall, to experience falling, and to think about, talk about, and write about how they felt when they fell? What if falling were an explicit part of the democratic project of schooling, on the one hand, and linked to the ways in which racial, cultural, and social justice are central and centered in our teaching and learning processes, on the other hand? What if falling were a pedagogical way of facilitating children, young people, and adults' critiques of racist institutional barriers that have long sought to hinder their academic success and engagement? What if falling were a strategic way of turning the gaze away from White, middle-class expectations and onto the heritage and community practices of children, youth, and families of color? What if . . .

These "what ifs" guided me as I read Bieler's book. I could not put it down. Instantly, I was drawn to her firsthand depictions of the four equity-oriented, justice-committed public high school English teachers she features: Jasmine Brown and Veronica James, two African American women; Melanie Davis, a Caribbean woman; and Heather Fredricks, a White woman, and the 9th- and 10th-grade students with whom they taught. Not only were they new English teachers working with new high school students, but they— Ms. Brown, Ms. James, Ms. Davis, and Ms. Fredricks—were committed to culturally relevant, responsive, and critical pedagogies. In fact, the ways they interacted with and acknowledged students before, during, and after class speak to their commitment to not having children fall or fail. How they talked about educational inequities and what Bieler named the "systemic influence of under-resourced schools, poverty, [and] the school-to-prison pipeline," point to a commitment to working against such inequities to ensure students are successful and teachers are supported to engage in equity-oriented, justice-driven interactions.

Thank you, Deb, for providing me an opportunity to learn with the teachers and students with whom you collaborated. Thank you for this beautiful, rich, and powerful text!

—Valerie Kinloch,
Renée and Richard Goldman Dean and professor,
School of Education, University of Pittsburgh

Acknowledgments

First, thank you, Jesus, creator and sustainer of all life and peace, for demonstrating how to love and how to interact with others, particularly those who have been marginalized. I could not have written this book without you.

I offer endless thanks and so much love to the real-life Heather, Jasmine, Melanie, and Veronica for welcoming me into your classrooms. I will always be grateful for your thoughtfulness, your generosity, and your inspiration.

To the 125 students, their families, building administrators, and district administrators in the actual Alpha, Cooper, Sampler, and Young high schools, please accept my deepest gratitude for your trust, kindness, and hospitality.

Thank you, NETS teachers, for honestly sharing your joys, struggles, and questions. I am deeply grateful to you for demonstrating the power of women organized to create change and to do so with even greater resolve after somebody calls your meetings "tea parties."

To Barbara Duszak, thank you for your brilliance and compassion especially during the first months at Sampler. To you and all of the research assistants who assisted with transcribing and coding—Abbi Billingsley, Lei Chen, Nicole Cheikh, Dan Greenland, Anthony Natoli, and Valerie Shinas—thank you. Thank you, Kristen Boylan, for the amazing cover photos!

For thoughtful, critical feedback on grant proposals many years ago that helped shape my early thinking about this research, thank you, Elizabeth Burr Moje, Ruth Curran Neild, and Kathy Schultz.

Thank you to wonderful friends and colleagues who have encouraged me in word, deed, and example—Maggie Andersen, Mollie Blackburn, Heyward Brock, Carol Burger, Joan DelFattore, Alison Dover, Kira Baker-Doyle, John Ernest, Jill Ewing Flynn, Carol Henderson, Mary Juzwik, Stephanie Kerschbaum, David Kirkland, Fran Koch, Jeanine Staples, Melva Ware, Kelly Wissman, and Jessica Pandya Zacher. To Anne Burns Thomas and Lalitha Vasudevan, PDSG (kc) always. To Valerie Kinloch, Marc Lamont Hill, and Linda Christensen, I appreciate your kindness, generosity, and friendship more than I can express.

Lots of love to the amazing students and alumni of the University of Delaware English Education @UD_XEE program! (#XEEproud!)

Thank you to the Noise-Canceling Headphones—Barbara Raudonis, Laura Talamante, Melissa Moorman, and David Cook—and to National Center for Faculty Development and Diversity founder Kerry Ann Rockquemore.

I am grateful to my Friday Women's Bible Study sisters; Pastor Bo Matthews; my Circle sisters Susan Cathcart, Sandy Dobbs, and Beverly Ford; the Concord Soccer family; and everyone at Brew HaHa, the best coffee/community in Delaware—free publicity, boom!—for all of your support and love.

Thanks to the NNeRD writing group (Nadia Behizadeh, Noah Asher Golden, and Rob Petrone) for your careful reading of, thoughtful responses to, and enthusiasm especially about early versions of Chapters 2 and 3.

To Emily Spangler, my anonymous reviewers, Susan Liddicoat, and everyone at Teachers College Press, thank you for believing in this project and for guiding its development with kindness and wisdom. It has been a privilege to work with you, and this work is infinitely better because of you.

Michele Evans Smith, thank you for encouraging me with your abiding example and with every bird and butterfly you've sent my way. I love and miss you so much.

To my parents, Ed and Lucille (Heist) Hillegass, thank you for loving, nurturing, teaching, believing in, encouraging, and supporting me. I could never express how grateful I am for the steadfast examples you have provided of how to live: walking with the Lord, working hard, and giving to others—all with humor and joy. I love you! Dad, thank you for teaching me some of the most important lessons I ever learned on that life-changing Killington hike—and for continuing to be one of the best teachers I know.

I would like to honor my late grandparents, Mary (Gall) and Paul Heist, and Kathryn (Nyemscek) and Clifford Hillegass, and all of my ancestors, for their sacrifices and legacies that opened so many doors to me. Thank you, also, to everyone in my extended family—the Bielers, Fishers, Hildebrands, and Vias—for your love and support.

Hi, Kim and Jordan, are you still reading this? I love you both so much! Did you notice that on the Dedication page, Jordan's name is first, but here, Kim's name is first? Well, Jordan, you know, it's an even-numbered year, and so that's why your name is first, first. Kim, can you please give me permission not to have to write another book that is published in an odd-numbered year in which your name is first, first? Thanks! And thank you for all of your smiles, hugs, kisses, laughs, cards, gifts, and love as I've worked on this book. I know I tell you this all the time, but I am SO happy I get to be your mom! I love you! (Also, NWCGAD, I hope!!!)

Scott, you have remained by my side for better and for worse, through sickness and health, for real. Thank you for the many sacrifices you made that enabled me to complete this project over its very long life; for reassuring me when I was discouraged; and for celebrating every step with me. I love you.

I also wish to express gratitude to those who generously funded this project:

- The ELATE/Conference on English Education (CEE) Research Initiative,
- The National Council of Teachers of English (NCTE) Research Foundation,
- The University of Delaware College of Arts and Sciences,
- The University of Delaware Department of English,
- The University of Delaware Faculty Enrichment Research Fund for Arts and Humanities,
- The University of Delaware Graduate Program Innovation and Improvement Grant, and
- The University of Delaware Office of the Provost.

CHAPTER 1

Introduction
Teacher/Student Interactions, Retention, and Equity

With 2 minutes until the bell rings to start her next class, Veronica's presence in the hallway outside her classroom door is the center of a whirlwind.[1]

"Vishon, pull your pants up," she laughingly calls down the hall. Vishon turns to face her, shaking his head—and pulling up his pants—as he continues walking to his next class.

"Miss J, do you have any snacks for me today?" Chanel asks.

"Um, yeah, I do, but they're downstairs. Come back right before lunch, and I'll walk down with you," Veronica responds. The student smiles, nods, and walks away.

"Where's your red lipstick?" Veronica asks one of the 9th graders approaching her. "I loved that color on you yesterday." The student smiles shyly and heads inside.

"Miss J, do you know where my portfolio is?" a student from one of her earlier classes yells over the noise from across the hall.

"Yeah, I think it's in the class bin. You were going to revise that poem, right?" Veronica responds. The student's face registers a flash of recognition, and she crosses the hall to retrieve it from Veronica's classroom.

"Can I go to the bathroom?" Tommy needs to know, barely slowing as he speed-walks toward her.

"Go, go, make it quick," says Veronica, glancing at the hallway clock. He picks up his pace walking away from the classroom.

Veronica sticks her head into the classroom after a large group of students arrives, announcing, "Sit in your writing groups today!" The students redirect themselves, and some who were already seated get up and move to new seats.

"Where were you yesterday?" Veronica is back in the hallway, directing her attention to Ceyonne, who seems to be dragging herself toward her.

"I was sick," she explains. "I'm still not feeling great. Can I have a pass to the nurse?"

---

1. All names of people and places are pseudonyms, and some details have been changed to ensure confidentiality.

1

"Hmm," Veronica says. "Just head down there now. You still have time before the bell."

"All right, thanks," Ceyonne mumbles back over her shoulder as she ambles away.

"Feel better!" Veronica says hopefully.

A worried-looking student approaches Veronica from inside the classroom and asks, "Are we having a notebook check today?" She shakes her head no, and he exhales with relief. "I left mine at home. Whew!" He dances back into the room.

"Can I get a drink?" inquires Rob, who also is coming back out of the classroom and into the hallway after putting his backpack down on his desk.

"Yeah, go ahead. Good morning, Khalil. What team do you play today?" she asks, pointing to the school lacrosse shirt he's wearing.

"Southern. It's gonna be freezing." Khalil grimaces as he passes her.

"Yeah, well, my excuse for not coming is that I'm staying for extra help today." She smiles.

As Veronica looks away from Khalil, she spies Diego sitting on top of his desk. "Diego! Sit! In your seat!" Diego snaps to attention, then slides into his chair. In the classroom, some students stand in front of the board, reading Veronica's instructions for today's journal; some are talking; others get their journals out of their backpacks. Veronica turns her attention back to the hallway.

"Hi, JJ! Hey, Taiye!" She greets two more students entering the room.

"Hey," they reply.

"Dan—please tell me you brought your essay for me today," she says to the student behind them.

"Yep," he replies.

"Nice." Veronica nods as he passes her, and the bell rings.

"How's my favorite teacher?" yells a former student to Veronica from far down the hall.

"Missing my favorite student, of course. But get to class!" She smiles, turns toward her classroom, and enters, pulling the door closed behind her. Without missing a beat on the way to her desk, she starts class even before the door shuts. "Good morning, everyone. You can go ahead and get started on your journals, and when I call your name, come on up and get your paper. I finished grading them all last night."

Dear reader, are you exhausted yet? If you are, then you have successfully taken a brief vicarious walk in a public high school English teacher's shoes. The mind-spinning pace of an ever-changing slate of student interactions is familiar territory for teachers. In fact, the vignette above, which occurred in a span of only 3 minutes, actually contains 15 separate teacher/student interactions.

That's five interactions per minute, or one interaction every 12 seconds. Allow that to sink in—because it is the average pace of the 15,287 interactions I observed between teachers and students during a 2-year study, across four teachers in four different schools. Back-and-forth talk between teachers and students is the cornerstone of all education, and while the high frequency and quick pace of teacher/student interactions are noteworthy enough, this book contends that the content of these interactions is also highly consequential for both teachers and students.

THE RETENTION CURRICULUM OF INTERACTIONS

In this book, I argue that when teachers interact with students, they not only are engaging in discourse about subject matter or personal matters; they are teaching students how much the students are (or are not) noticed and valued, and whether school is a place in which students want to stay. At the same time, in these interactions, the teachers themselves also are determining whether they want to stay in schools. In this way, I suggest that every interaction between a teacher and a student constantly shapes, as well as reflects, both participants' attitudes about staying in school. For new high school teachers and their students alike, these attitudes are unstable, continually shifting with every teacher/student interaction. At any given moment, a teacher's or student's *positioning toward retention*—a current sense of commitment to remaining a teacher or a student—can be observed in voiced or visual expressions of praise, pleasure, efficacy, inefficacy, or frustration with classroom experiences, as well as in direct references to staying in or leaving school. This book details how, in their numerous daily interactions with one another, teachers and students are always positioning themselves either toward or away from retention and revealing this position. Over time, these attitudes begin to solidify, and both teachers and students eventually make decisions about staying in school.

> Teachers typically engage in five student interactions per minute—that's one interaction every 12 seconds. Each one shapes and reflects participants' attitudes about staying in school.

In the hallway before her class began, Veronica engaged in important teaching and learning about retention with her students. The instruction she directed at Vishon let him know that he was noticed, and her laugh communicated that she supported him. When she complimented a nonbinary student's lipstick, expressed support for Ceyonne regarding her illness, and talked about lacrosse with Khalil, Veronica taught these students that she was paying attention to the details of their lives and was building relationships with them (see Figure 1.1). And when she helped a student locate her portfolio to revise a poem, responded to a student's question about a notebook check, and asked Daniel whether he brought his finished essay, she was teaching her students that they could succeed

Figure 1.1. Noticing to Build Relationships

Teachers can learn to observe their students closely (column 1), use conversation starters in the moment (column 2), and then continue building on them over time.

When there is something different or noteworthy about a student's appearance (e.g., a new haircut or outfit, a sports uniform) . . .	• "You look so nice today!" • "Let me see your new haircut—it looks nice." • "Is the game at home today?"
When a student has returned to school (e.g., after an illness or a trip) . . .	• "Hey, are you feeling any better today? • "I missed you." • "How was your trip?"
When a student has decorated something (e.g., their notebook or backpack) . . .	• "What does your button say?" • "Did you draw that?"
When a student is singing, rapping, or humming . . .	• Join them! • "What song is that?"
When students are showing fatigue (e.g., their head is on their desk, or they are yawning) . . .	• "Are you feeling okay?" • "Didn't get enough sleep last night?"

and that she wanted to help them do just that. In this teaching, Veronica also created herself as someone who held important knowledge, used that knowledge to assist and connect individually with her students, and established a welcoming environment—all actions that teachers can take to help their students stay and succeed in school. In these particular before-class interactions, Veronica was not "teaching English" in the traditional sense, as she was not focused on teaching her content-area curriculum. But, I argue, there is another "curriculum" that is present in all teacher/student interactions, both those that are explicitly related to subject matter and those that are not: what teachers and students are learning about their "fit" with, or sense of belonging to, school.

Most of today's conversations about public education in America focus on major issues such as policies, standards, curriculum, assessments, student demographics, teacher preparation, parent support, school resources, and school leadership. All of these important variables shape teachers' daily practice enormously. But even as policies change, as new assessments are required, as schools' resources grow or diminish, as other innumerable variables fluctuate, the central and defining feature of education persists: Students and teachers will always be interacting in the midst of it all, and they will always be positioning themselves toward or away from retention in and through these interactions. The great potential of these interactions to change lives for the better is often why students love school, why people become teachers, and why both students and teachers stay in school. Yet, while we as teachers rightly conceptualize interactions as vehicles for teaching students content-based knowledge and skills and productive behaviors and dispositions, the significance of interactions in shaping our own and students' retention is typically far from our day-to-day radar. However, I argue, teachers and teacher educators can work toward increased student and teacher retention when they are mindful of the power of interactions to shape such decisions.

This work is urgent, as all across America, many students and teachers are choosing not to stay in school: Between 40 and 50% of new teachers quit within the first 5 years (Ingersoll & Strong, 2011), and between 20 and 30% of students drop out annually, with much higher percentages among teachers and students of color and in other marginalized groups (Balfanz et al., 2014; Bowers, Sprott, & Taff, 2013; Heckman & Lafontaine, 2010; Ingersoll & Connor, 2009; Ingersoll & May, 2011; Snyder & Dillow, 2011). These worrisome trends exacerbate the under-representation of experienced teachers of color and of graduates of color. The economic costs of these losses are also daunting: Teacher attrition has cost $2.2 billion annually (Borman & Dowling, 2008), and student dropout $154 billion (Alliance for Excellent Education, 2011). Increasing the retention of marginalized students, and the retention of their teachers, is a critical social justice issue, and not only for these reasons. When marginalized students stay in school, they have a greater chance to emerge skillful and critically literate and powerful, to go to college, to earn a higher income. When their teachers stay longer in the profession, they have a greater chance to increase their effectiveness as they instruct students to become skillful, critically literate, and powerful; to enjoy the benefits of deepening their roots; to invest in a community long enough to help make it better. Student dropout and teacher attrition prevent full emergence from occurring; they are like a late-season frost that wilts delicate spring blossoms. When students and teachers remain in school, there is a greater chance that they can use their more deeply developed skills and knowledge to create a more equitable world for themselves and for others.

EQUITY-ORIENTED TEACHERS: A DEFINITION

Equity-oriented teachers understand that historical legacies of inequity play out every day in schools, and they commit to both shielding students from the damaging effects of these legacies and working to dismantle them. What are historical legacies of inequity? They are pervasive systems, policies, and

practices that function to maintain the unequal status of and unequal resources for different groups of people. These legacies aim to protect the status quo, in which people who enjoy wealth and power retain such privileges,
and people who currently do not have such privileges have no viable pathways toward them. In the sphere of education, the persistence of these legacies can be seen, for example, in the underfunding of schools in communities
struggling with poverty; the hyper-punitive approach to school discipline in
urban schools that criminalizes youth of color; the "achievement gap" (as
opposed to the "opportunity gap") narrative that positions marginalized
youth as chronically underachieving; or curriculum and instruction that
position White people's language, achievements, or texts as the norm or
the standard. In other words, equity-oriented teachers align their perspectives and practices with the notion of equity; they view students, families,
communities, schools, texts, practices—everything—through an equity lens.
They look for and take opportunities to actively promote and increase equity wherever they can.

Equity-oriented teachers are thus distinct from other loving, caring,
well-meaning teachers. While members of the latter group often see themselves as functioning purely as individuals or only within the realm of their
unique environment, equity-oriented teachers see themselves and their students as participants in a much larger, historic struggle. While well-meaning
teachers obviously can and do work for good and make important differences in the lives of their students, equity-oriented teachers aim to focus
their efforts primarily on doing the most good and making the most difference in the lives of historically marginalized students. Well-meaning
teachers may be troubled by inequities they observe—like fewer students
of color in the gifted program or in honors or AP classes at their school;
or required novels featuring people of color only in marginalized or oppressed roles; or higher absence, tardiness, detention, or suspension rates
among students from particular neighborhoods. Yet these teachers may
doubt their ability to effect change or may avert their eyes in order to
avoid "getting too political." Well-meaning teachers may make some equity-oriented moves but not necessarily or intentionally be part of the movement. However, as Emdin (2016) compellingly explains, teachers' good
intentions ultimately can still prove harmful to marginalized youth: "As
long as white middle-class teachers are recruited to schools occupied by
urban youth of color, without any consideration of how they affirm and
reestablish power dynamics that silence students, issues that plague urban
education . . . will persist" (p. 9).

Efforts to conceptualize equity-oriented teaching also can benefit from
service learning scholarship—particularly Mitchell's (2008) work, which
differentiates "traditional service learning" from "critical service learning."
In the traditional model, volunteers help meet a community need and reflect

on their experiences. However, in the critical model, while volunteers still help meet a community need, they do so while examining injustices that may have caused this need, working to empower community members and engaging in nonhierarchical partnerships. The notion of traditional versus critical service learning offers an important parallel for traditional (well-meaning) versus critical (equity-oriented) teaching. This distinction is not meant to disparage any teacher's effort to meet individual students' needs but rather to urge all teachers to be more mindful of the role they are already playing in schools—and to encourage teachers to leverage their individual and collective power toward increasing equity for disadvantaged youth. Such an orientation is urgently needed.

For equity-oriented teachers, interactions—as well as all other aspects of their practice—are never inconsequential; they are understood as having the potential to contribute to or change cycles of inequity. As the conceptual framework provided in Figure 1.2 illustrates, for social justice– and equity-oriented teachers, the vast universe of teacher moves, which includes interactions—like their dispositions, relationships with students, curriculum choices, and pedagogical practices—is a natural outgrowth of their beliefs about inequity and commitment to working toward a more equitable, just world. This intentionally multicultural conceptual framework illustrates important commonalities underlying the work of scholars who may:

- Use different terminology (e.g., social justice, equity, diversity, multicultural, anti-racist);
- Emphasize different forms of inequity (e.g., race, ethnicity, class) or spaces in which inequity occurs (e.g., urban, the school-to-prison pipeline); or
- Focus on different lenses or ways forward (e.g., critical race theory, critical consciousness, critical literacy, urban literacies, racial literacy, culturally sustaining pedagogy).

While critically conscious teachers may focus, at any given time, on better aligning particular aspects of their practice with their beliefs, they share a mostly unstated goal of ensuring that as many of their practices, with as many of their students, as often as possible, are in harmony with their beliefs. They see themselves as intentionally acting as change agents toward the empowerment of people of color and members of other subordinated groups (Collins, 2000; Kumashiro, 2004). Equity-oriented teachers' practices can re-create schools as places in which students' identities and voices are valued, and this work, particularly when it is done with marginalized or minoritized students, can be revolutionary.

Figure 1.2. Conceptual Framework for Social Justice– and Equity-Oriented Teachers

Worldview: What Is Wrong in the World?

- *Conscientização:* Oppressors "perpetuate injustice" by dehumanizing the oppressed, who must take action to humanize themselves through praxis ("reflection and action upon the world in order to transform it") (Freire, 1970/2000, pp. 44, 51).
- *Critical race theory:* Race should be "foreground[ed . . .] as an explanatory tool for the persistence of inequality" (Ladson-Billings, 1997, p. 132).

View of Schools: How Does This Play out in Schools?

- Schools are inequitably funded, with those in poorer communities of color being persistently, severely under-resourced (Kozol, 1991).
- A "hidden curriculum" running throughout students' experiences in school reproduces a system of unequal social classes (Anyon, 1980).
- Groups of students and teachers experience inequity via a process of minoritization (Benitez, 2010).
- Poverty, resource distribution, and institutional racism inhibit minoritized students' educational success (Picower, 2012).
- Students of color and students in poverty are criminalized in schools (Wald & Losen, 2003) and pushed out (Morris, 2016).

View of Teachers' Role: How Can Teachers Play a Part in Responding to and Changing These Realities?

- Understand that teaching is political (Freire, 1970/2000) and that teachers are political beings (Ladson-Billings, 1994) and social actors (Dover, 2013).
- Because schools reproduce inequity, work toward halting this reproduction (Weis & Fine, 2005) and engage in a collective struggle against the status quo (Ladson-Billings, 1994) and toward the empowerment of people of color and other subordinated groups (Collins, 1998, 2000; Kumashiro, 2004).
- Raise student awareness of injustice and inequity (Dover, 2013) and explicitly address how to challenge them (Normore, 2008).

Figure 1.2. Conceptual Framework for Social Justice– and Equity-Oriented Teachers (continued)

- Be guided by a critically conscious purpose and a sense of duty to students and the community (Duncan-Andrade, 2007).
- "Enable [students] to develop the critical analytical tools necessary to understand oppression and their own socialization within oppressive systems, and to develop a sense of agency and capacity to interrupt and change oppressive patterns and behaviors in themselves and in the institutions and communities of which they are a part" (Bell, 2007, p. 2).
- "Facilitate healing and transformation" (Fujiyoshi, 2015, p. 5).
- "Improve race relations; help all students acquire the knowledge, attitudes, skills needed to participate in cross-cultural interactions and in personal, social, and civic action that will help make our nation more democratic and just" (Banks, 2007, p. xii).

View of Teacher Moves:
How Exactly Can Teachers Enact These Commitments?

Dispositions

- Teach with a belief in all students' brilliance, joy, and a commitment to justice (Christensen, 2009).
- Trust the people (Freire, 1970/2000).
- Be humble, knowing that there is always more to learn (Duncan-Andrade, 2007).
- Practice love, which manifests as a commitment to others and is "the key to leaving behind anger, negativity, and hopelessness" (Fujiyoshi, 2015, p. 5).
- Embody a spirit of hopefulness (Ayers, 2004) and care (Cassidy & Bates, 2005).
- Continually assess whether and how you may be reproducing hegemony and actively avoid doing so (A. Willis et al., 2008).
- Approach students, particularly students of color or other marginalized students, as a warm demander (Ware, 2006).

Curriculum

- Engage in multicultural education as an anti-racist act (Nieto, 1999).
- Help students develop their voices and support them as they use their voices to connect with others (hooks, 1994) and to work

Figure 1.2. Conceptual Framework for Social Justice– and Equity-Oriented Teachers (continued)

toward fighting injustice and restructuring oppressive systems (Collins, 1998).

- Draw on students' funds of knowledge (Moll, Amanti, Neff, & Gonzalez, 1992) and an asset (not deficit) perspective.
- Create for your students "opportunities to survive and thrive" from a place of "love that can help us see your young people as a whole versus broken when they enter schools" (Paris & Alim, 2017).
- Participate in a broad spectrum of literacy that incorporates both written and spoken texts (Ladson-Billings, 1994).
- "[Provide] young people with tools to critique and question the world around them as they make sense of texts, including those mediated by the school environment and by popular and media texts" (Haddix & Rojas, 2011, p. 115).
- Use diverse languages and texts (Lee, 2007).

Pedagogical Practices

- Use culturally sustaining pedagogy "to perpetuate and foster—to sustain—linguistic, literate, and cultural pluralism" (Paris, 2012, p. 93).
- Maintain a supportive climate that embraces multiple perspectives; emphasizes critical thinking and inquiry; and promotes academic, civil, and personal growth (Dover, 2013).
- "Shift and expand the definition of literacy practices, introduce counternarratives to traditional power discourses that frame diversities as deficits . . . , and explicitly address issues of discrimination, race, and power within the literacy curriculum capitalizing on the [students'] experiences" (Haddix & Price-Dennis, 2013, p. 275).
- Engage in tremendous preparation for classes (Duncan-Andrade, 2007).
- "[Protect] students from the threat of internalizing negative stereotypes" by teaching racial literacy, "the ability to read, recast, and resolve racially stressful social interactions" (Stevenson, 2014, p. 4).
- "Recognize, respond to, and redress conditions that deny some students access to the educational opportunities enjoyed by their peers and . . . sustain equitable learning environments for all students" (Gorski, 2013, p. 19).

Relationships with Students

- View and treat students with respect and dignity (hooks, 1994).

Figure 1.2. Conceptual Framework for Social Justice– and Equity-Oriented Teachers (continued)

- Treat students as subjects, not objects; as partners in teaching and learning (Freire, 1970/2000).
- Engage in organic, democratic solidarity with students; and understand that democracy is always in flux and rife with paradoxes (DeStigter, 2008).
- Affirm, celebrate minoritized students' culture; provide academic support for them and promote a positive view of them; apprentice students into a learning community rather than teaching in isolated or unrelated ways; legitimize real-life experiences and include as part of the official curriculum (Ladson-Billings, 1994).
- Distinctly commit to building trust with students; love and support them with high expectations, yet be indignant about student failure (Duncan-Andrade, 2007).

THE ROLE OF EQUITY-ORIENTED TEACHERS IN RETENTION

As stated earlier, the main argument of this book is that enacting a commitment to equity and social justice in teacher/student interactions has retention power for both teachers and students. Because equity-oriented, critically conscious teachers believe that inequities exist in American society and that teachers can play a key role in working toward justice, these teachers are a particularly valuable population to investigate for insights about both student and teacher retention. They take upon themselves a personal responsibility for student success even while acknowledging the massive, systemic influence of under-resourced schools, poverty, the school-to-prison pipeline, and cultures of violence.

Equity-oriented teaching practices can yield many benefits other than just increased educational retention, of course; for example, they improve the quality of students' and teachers' lived experiences in schools, and deepen learning by connecting concepts to students' lives and to real-world scenarios. Equity-oriented teachers are aware that all aspects of their teaching—from their curriculum and assessments to their interactions with students—are political acts, as each of these teaching decisions holds the potential to value and empower youth, to help them raise their consciences and voices, or to discourage or silence them. By closely examining equity-oriented teachers' interactions with students, I hope both to help all teachers interact with marginalized students in ways that create strong ties to school and to increase the number of teachers who commit to doing so as an important part of their professional practice.

Retaining equity-oriented teachers in American public schools is critical for our country's future, as suggested by the statistics I reported earlier. In this book, I provide ways for teachers, new and experienced, to be aware of and intentional about how they enact their commitment to equity in their interactions with students and how they can harness the retention power of these interactions, from their classroom décor to their banter in the moments before and after class. I also propose that in order to retain equity-oriented teachers and their students in public high school classrooms, theories and pedagogies that prioritize social justice must become central to teacher preparation and educational practice.

But what happens when new, equity-oriented teachers enter the profession intending to enact a commitment to social justice in their interactions with students? How do they actually talk with the students about whose success they are most concerned? Are there any patterns that their talk typically takes? Where can we see teachers and students positioning themselves toward retention in these interactions? To answer these questions, I examined how four new, equity-oriented public high school English teachers—Jasmine Brown and Veronica James, African American women; Melanie Davis, a Caribbean woman; and Heather Fredricks, a White woman—interacted with the 9th and 10th graders who were not faring well in their classes. New English teachers are disproportionately assigned to teach both lower grade and lower track levels (Bieler, Holmes, & Wolfe, 2017), and these four women were no exception to this trend. The book's focus on 9th and 10th grades shines a light on a critical space in which both new high school teachers' and new high school students' decisions to stay in school are made and revealed through conversation.

THE ROLE OF CONTEXTS

In this book, I examine teacher/student interactions through a sociocultural lens, in which learning is understood to be social and cultural in nature, created as individuals change and are changed by the multiple contexts they inhabit (Holland, Lachicotte, Skinner, & Cain, 1998; Lave & Wenger, 1991). In this view, contexts clearly matter, and they can help explain, for example, when and how new, equity-oriented teachers are able to realize their commitments through their interactions with students, and when they are not.

School Culture

In a theory of teacher/student interactions and retention that I discuss throughout the book, local contexts greatly influence the likelihood that (and the ease with which) critically conscious educators will interact with their students in ways that are consistent with their beliefs. Specifically, this likelihood is related to a school's location along a spectrum from, on one end, hosting a negative pushout culture to, on the other end, embracing a positive, supportive culture—what I call a *pull-in culture*.

Pushout culture refers to the negative environment (Fine, 1991) and criminalization of students (Morris, 2016) in some schools that persistently "push" students "out" in ways that are central to the school-to-prison pipeline (Dignity in Schools, 2011). It is important to distinguish between the terms *dropout* and *pushout*. The first term, *dropout*, implicitly assigns blame to students and suggests that they agentively either directly make a decision to leave school or make choices that indirectly result in their leaving school. The second term, *pushout*, refers to "a student who feels forced out of school not just due to harsh discipline, but because of unsupportive teachers and staff, overcrowding, lack of safety, rigid test-driven curriculum, inadequate resources, and lack of student support services" (Harris, 2010). In other words, the term *dropout* locates the problem of student attrition in the individual student, whereas the term *pushout* locates it in micro- and macro-level policies and systems. In schools with a pushout culture, feelings of fear and hopelessness can be common among both students and teachers. Other markers of negative culture for teachers and students include being unable to enact their agency; being negatively perceived and/or perceiving others negatively; being preoccupied with being disciplined; and experiencing a sense of stress, insecurity, failure, illness, isolation, or apathy. In fact, teacher/student interactions occupy a point of tension between teachers' social justice commitment and the pushout culture of schools; that is, when teachers interact with students in ways that are consistent with an equity orientation, they are acting in direct opposition to a school's pushout culture. In its most egregious forms, pushout culture can be so powerful that it makes such interactions almost impossible; yet, when teachers do succeed in cultivating equity-oriented interactions with their students in such environments, they chip away at the toxic culture surrounding them. However, because great effort is expended in going against the grain in schools where pushout culture reigns, teacher attrition forces are particularly strong, and teacher burnout is common.

On the other end of the spectrum, positive and nurturing school cultures include supportive people, practices, policies, and/or structures for students' and teachers' success. Markers of positive culture in supportive schools include teachers and students experiencing a sense of agency (Bieler, 2004, 2010, 2013), connection or belonging, accomplishment or success, and peace or wellness. In these supportive schools, equity-oriented teachers enjoy less resistance to their efforts to contribute to a pull-in culture. As a result, they interact with students in ways that are consistent with their beliefs, increasing the likelihood that these teachers will engage in critical practices, that they will remain long-term teachers, and that their marginalized students will remain in school and graduate.

In Figure 1.3, I illustrate this theory of teacher/student interactions and retention with a diagram based on physics principles and featuring two levers, each with a base pivoting on a fulcrum. Using physics terminology, when teachers apply the "effort" of an equity commitment to the lever at

Figure 1.3. Teacher/Student Interaction and Retention Theory

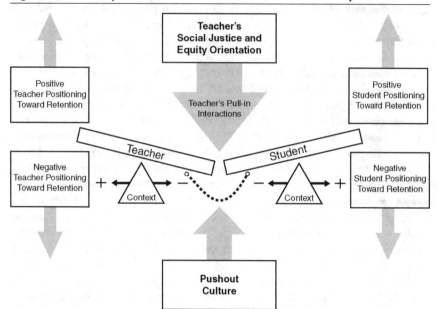

the point of connection between teachers and students, the "load" of positioning to retention is lifted or made positive for both students and teachers. When this "effort" is not applied, positionings to retention are static. However, when pushout culture is the primary factor influencing teacher/student interactions, positionings toward retention are lowered or made negative. Similarly, when the fulcrum gets closer to the "load," depicted here at the outside location of "positioning toward retention," less "effort" is needed to overcome this "load"; this "decrease of the load arm" is known as the "mechanical advantage." (This is why, for example, if you have trouble cutting a flower stem when you place it at the far end of a pair of scissors, you have success when you "decrease the load arm" by moving the stem closer to the point where the blades come together, at the fulcrum.) Overall, when the majority of contexts in which teachers and students are involved, provides positive support, less "effort" is required of teacher/student interactions to increase positioning toward retention. When their contexts, overall, are not supportive and the fulcrum slides inward, much greater "effort" is required from teachers to increase positioning toward retention.

Teacher Tenure

Another important contextual factor that affects teachers' engagement in equity-oriented practice is the traditional teacher tenure system. Because equity-oriented practices often involve questioning or resisting common practices, they entail some professional risk to teachers, even those in supportive environments. Pre-tenured teachers, who are typically in their first 3 or 4 years of teaching, are understandably more hesitant to take such risks. The hesitancy of new, equity-oriented teachers can differ from that of well-meaning teachers because it has a shelf life: New, equity-oriented teachers sometimes seem to be (im)patiently biding their time before they can spring into action. Sometimes, pre-tenured equity-oriented teachers can look a lot like well-meaning teachers. What is different, though—and what I can attest to from many years of working with new teachers—is that often, pre-tenured equity-oriented teachers silently experience profound distress when they witness inequities but cannot disrupt them because the nature of their job is so all-consuming that they cannot find time or energy to do so (Bieler & Young, forthcoming) and/or because they fear that they may lose their job if they try to step in.

This state of being is not sustainable, and it causes many new, equity-oriented teachers to turn their backs on their dreams of becoming a teacher and on their years of training, and leave the classroom once and for all. Worse, it is during these first 3 to 4 years of teaching that teachers are most likely to be assigned to teach the most vulnerable students—for example, as I pointed out earlier, new public high school English teachers are disproportionately assigned to teach lower level or 9th- and 10th-grade classes, as opposed to higher level or 11th- and 12th-grade classes. When we consider that (1) equity-oriented teachers often wait to take professional risks for equity until after their first 3 or 4 years; (2) during these very years, teachers are most likely to be assigned to teach marginalized students; and (3) 40–50% of new teachers quit within the first 5 years, we easily can see the urgent need for new teachers to learn how to engage immediately in equity-oriented teaching practices that pave a solid retention path both for themselves and for their students.

> Often, pre-tenured equity-oriented teachers silently experience profound distress caused by the inequities they witness and their perception that if they try to step in, they will lose their job.

THE NETS CONTEXT

This book examines the interactions that four new public high school English teachers who entered the profession with commitments to equity had with the 9th- and 10th-grade students about whose success they were most concerned. These four teachers participated in the New English Teachers for Social Justice Project (NETS), an action research group I created and facilitated between 2006 and 2010. They all earned undergraduate degrees from the same secondary English teacher preparation program, where they regularly expressed and exhibited commitments to social justice as they learned about pedagogies that are culturally relevant (Ladson-Billings, 1995a), culturally responsive (Gay, 2000), anti-racist (Delpit, 2006), and critical (Freire, 1970/2000; Peterson, 1999), and where I served as their professor. They and 10 other new teachers met voluntarily at my home for several years one Saturday morning a month during the school year and over periodic summer weekend retreats. One NETS teacher, Jamie, summarized the group's working definition of social justice when she explained that teachers joined NETS because they wanted to "'[make] changes' in schools and in society at large, 'so that all individuals are afforded an equal opportunity to succeed'" (Bieler, 2011, p. 4). I hoped that NETS would provide a place of support and a basis for action for these new public school teachers, and that by pooling their experiences, they could better understand and work collectively to change the inequities they encountered. Together, we conducted two phases of inquiry that eventually led us, in the third phase, to the focus of this book.

Phase One: Exploring Teacher Narratives

During the first phase of NETS, the teachers and I worked to define the dimensions of "teaching for social justice" among members of our group to determine how to proceed in our work together. The teachers narrated many experiences that they believed illustrated social justice issues in their classrooms, departments, schools, and communities. Our group's focus became "students who are falling through the cracks"—students whom the new teachers felt they were unable to reach, despite their best efforts, and a term used by Lawrence-Lightfoot (1983) in her seminal portrait of American high schools. Ironically, as the teachers worked to determine the range and variation of students in this category and narrated numerous examples of how and why they seemed not to be meeting these students' various needs, they came to realize that as new teachers, they, too, were in danger of "falling through the cracks" of the profession. A guiding question for NETS emerged from the last line of the following narrative, which Jamie wrote at the beginning of her second year as an urban English teacher:

> Erica was a bright, cheerful girl who told me the first day that English was her favorite subject. She stopped coming in November. "Speak to Erica" and "Call Erica's mother" remained on my to-do list until December, at which point it was too late. It just kept getting pushed back, pushed back, because of the craziness of my daily schedule: I would try to make a quick phone call, but there would be trouble, and there'd be something that I had to do next, and then, all of a sudden, she disappeared, and I'm like, damn, you know? I

missed it. She's gone—she never came back to school. Period. I did see her afterwards, smoking in the park with the boys from the group home. I knew she was heading for trouble, and I silently watched my predictions unfold. I felt super guilty and I still do because there's a couple of kids who I really felt that I could have done something about. But how do you stop a child from falling when you're falling faster? (Bieler, 2011, p. 4)

Phase Two: Examining Teacher Assignments

As we continued to meet, the NETS teachers began to suspect that the almost-constant sense of failure they felt was, at least in part, due to the fact that, compared with their more experienced colleagues, they had been assigned to teach unusually large numbers of high-need students. They realized that while they as new teachers in their respective schools had been assigned to teach primarily lower track 9th- and 10th-grade students, their more experienced colleagues typically taught higher track and higher grade students. The overwhelming sense of failure with which they regarded their teaching, they felt, was not shared by their experienced colleagues, and we wondered whether the teacher assignment pattern we noticed within our group was an anomaly or symptomatic of a much larger trend.

We conducted a study in a stratified random sample of 50 districts across the five northern mid-Atlantic states (Delaware, Maryland, New Jersey, New York, and Pennsylvania) in which NETS members were teaching. Participants in the survey were teachers in 12 districts and all five states, representing five diverse locales from rural town to large city (Hoffman, 2007), and varying widely in promoting power, the percentage of 9th graders who graduate 4 years later (Balfanz & Letgers, 2004). We created a database of the 175 public high school English teachers' experience level and their 246 class assignments, and we surveyed their experiences and beliefs (Bandura, 2001). The study (Bieler et al., 2017) revealed that new English teachers indeed are disproportionately assigned to teach both lower grade and lower track levels. We also found that new English teachers are less likely than experienced English teachers to receive their assignment preferences. These findings, alongside the reality that most students who drop out do so before the end of 10th grade (Burris & Roberts, 2012), mean that new English teachers teach a much larger percentage of students who eventually will drop out than do more experienced high school English teachers. Given the common characteristics of students who go on to drop out, such as having low attendance and earning low grades, it follows that new high school English teachers spend much more time than their experienced peers contacting absent students' families/guardians, catching students up on missed work, creating and administering make-up quizzes and tests, and providing extra help on course content and skills.

Phase Three: "Working for Transformation in the Smallest Places"

As the NETS teachers continued to experience a constant sense of failing the students who seemed to need them the most, we talked often of the much-feared "burnout" experienced by new and justice-oriented teachers. We wondered:

- What can teachers do to catch students before they fall through the cracks?
- Where are teachers missing opportunities to do so, perhaps without even knowing it?
- What kinds of cracks do the students fall through, and how can teachers seal them?

We shifted the focus of our inquiry from factors primarily outside the classroom (e.g., administrators making assignments, teacher tracking) to life inside the teachers' classrooms. We became clearer in our understanding of teacher attrition, student failure, and student dropout as social justice issues.

We also realized that while research on teacher attrition (e.g., Boyd et al., 2011; Ingersoll, 2003) and research on student dropout (e.g., Lee & Burkham, 2003; Neild, Stoner-Eby, & Furstenberg, 2001) are consistently active areas of scholarly inquiry, the issues unfortunately have been considered in isolation from each other. Neither field has examined the interactions between new teachers and 9th and 10th graders, the very populations more likely than their peers to drop out of school. In fact, Neild et al. (2001) suggest that such analysis involving 9th graders is particularly desirable because their experience during this transition year significantly shapes their school retention path. The NETS teachers and I saw the need for new knowledge about what happens when equity-oriented teachers meet students in the "revolving door" of 9th- and 10th-grade English classes (Ingersoll, 2003). We believe that this knowledge is important because, as Maxine Greene (1998) has written, such meetings can help change the world:

> To teach for social justice is to teach for enhanced perception and imaginative explorations, for the recognition of social wrongs, of sufferings, of pestilences wherever and whenever they arise. It is to find models in literature and in history of the indignant ones, the ones forever ill at ease, and the loving ones who have taken the side of the victims of pestilences, whatever their names or places of origin. It is to teach so that the young may be awakened to the joy of working for transformation in the smallest places, so that they may become healers and change their worlds. (p. xlv)

We came to realize that we really needed to look deeply into their "smallest places," moments of interaction between members of these two populations—new teachers and their students who might be falling through the cracks. Specifically, we wanted to study the interactions of equity-oriented teachers who come to the profession with an awareness of injustice and a commitment to working against it—which often translates into committing extra time and effort to students who aren't thriving in the classroom. We knew that willpower alone is not enough to sustain new teachers' efforts to support marginalized students, and we knew that there was a need for research to establish how new teachers attempt to support vulnerable students and how these efforts affect their own career trajectory.

Research on how equity-oriented teaching is practiced during class time is especially important because, as one review of research on youth and risk (Vasudevan & Campano, 2009) notes, much of what we know about critically conscious teaching is based on scholarship that is based outside of school hours and/or school walls. In these settings, teachers have helped raise students' voices in elective courses (Wissman, 2007), after school (Fisher, 2007), during the summer (Morrell & Duncan-Andrade, 2005), or in drop-in programs like those based on June Jordan's Poetry for the People (Jocson, 2006). Portraits of equity-oriented teachers' practice during school hours, within required subjects like English, are rare by comparison, as the constraints therein are tremendous, and the need for such practice in compulsory settings is even more urgent. The constraints—from large class sizes and underfunding to required curriculum and emphasis on high-stakes, standardized tests—can deter teachers from engaging in equity-oriented practices. The inherent professional risks in confronting these constraints are significant, posing additional challenges for new teachers who are untenured. As a result, it is understandable that our field's most impactful scholarship on equity-oriented classroom teaching has focused more often on experienced teachers (e.g., Fecho, 2004; Foster, 1997; Ladson-Billings, 2005; Nieto, 2003) than on new teachers. A serious analysis of what it is that new teachers committed to social justice actually do in the classroom is needed to extend the impact of research on equity-oriented educational practice and policy.

This book seeks to fill these gaps in understanding in order to better prepare and support new, equity-oriented teachers; improve their success with the students who stand to gain the most from their attention; and uncover the range and complexity of these teacher/student interactions during the school day, in the classroom. I wish to offer to the teacher retention conversation a unique documentation and analysis of *firsthand, in vivo* classroom data rather than secondhand, or reported, classroom data. In this work, I am responding to Cochran-Smith's (2004b) call for research that examines "the conditions and contexts that sustain teachers' efforts to work for social justice as well as the conditions that constrain them" (p. 164) and to McCann, Johannessen, and Ricca's (2005) call for studies that rely on "actual observations" rather than stand-alone "descriptions of the actions that [teachers] *reported* they would take" in order to curb "the devastating loss to the profession of [talented new English teachers] and to the students whose lives they would affect" (pp. 164–165, emphasis in original). This book offers answers to important questions:

- How do new teachers committed to working for social justice within the boundaries of traditional public high school classes interact with the students about whose success they are most concerned?
- What are their common discourse patterns?
- How do both the teachers and the students create, or exhibit any signs of, their positioning toward retention during these interactions?
- What can we learn from these patterns that will help us improve the preparation and retention of culturally sustaining, justice-oriented teachers in our public schools?

A BRIEF DESCRIPTION OF RESEARCH METHODS

Teacher, School, and Student Participants

When we decided together to pursue the third phase of our work, all of the NETS teachers carefully considered how risky it would be for them to ask permission from their administrators to participate in this research, how much risk they personally were willing to take, and whether they were able to make time in their busy schedules to participate. For some, this process of deliberation did not take long, as they knew that the risks would be far too great in their context. For others, the process took longer, and some soul-searching was involved. In the end, seven NETS teachers expressed initial interest in participating; of these seven, two determined that they were too busy to participate, and five sought administrative permission to participate in the project. Of these five, one did not receive permission, and four—those teachers featured in this book—did receive permission. As Table 1.1 indicates, during the study, Melanie and Veronica were 1st-year teachers, Heather was a 3rd-year teacher, and Jasmine was a 4th-year teacher.

The four teachers' schools represented differing levels of diversity and a wide range of communities, including rural, suburban, and urban. The teachers chose to include in the study only classes in which all of the students were interested in participating and in which another teacher, such as a special education teacher, would not regularly be in the room. Altogether, seven classes, with a total of 125 students, were included in this project: five 9th-grade classes and two 10th-grade classes. In Heather's and Veronica's classes, the students' races/ethnicities were very similar to those of the overall school population, with 0% and 39% students of color, respectively. In Jasmine's and Melanie's classes, 96% of the students were students of color, a significantly higher percentage than those of the overall school population (40% and 70% students of color, respectively).

All four of the teachers on whom the book is based have now passed the critical 5-year mark. In fact, when this book went to press, they had gone well beyond that, having completed their 9th to 12th year in the classroom. Because these teachers have stayed in the classroom, our work provides rare insight into how, in their earliest years, and within the boundaries of traditional public high school classes, new, equity-oriented teachers help marginalized students succeed. As reported earlier, almost all portraits of equity-oriented teacher practice feature either experienced teachers or out-of-school settings. Because new teachers take professional risks when they work toward social justice in public high school classrooms, particularly when they are untenured, this book raises the visibility of new classroom teachers who are doing this important work and can help guide others who seek to join them.

Characteristics of Focal Students

Because we wanted to examine the interactions between the teachers and their "students who were falling through the cracks," we determined that the focal students would meet at least one of the following criteria at some point, as there was some movement in and out of the focal-student category:

- Have a D or an F average in English
- Engage in activities that research cites as indicative of high "at risk" for dropout—such as being absent frequently, not turning in work, not participating in class, and being disruptive
- Be someone that the English teacher felt she was not reaching despite her best efforts

These criteria were drawn from Schargel, Thacker, and Bell's (2007) study of school turnaround and affirmed in Feldman, Smith, and Waxman's (2017) study of high school dropouts' stories.

One of the first things we learned in this study is also one of the most important: As shown in Table 1.1, 47% of the students in these English teachers' classes were, in the teachers' estimation, "falling through the cracks." The finding that these teachers, across differing class sizes and student demographics, were consistently and extremely concerned about the success of *nearly half* of their students is stunning. In contrast, many new teachers, relying on their own schooling experiences, believe that most students are successful and that school comes easily to them (Lortie, 1975).

Table 1.1. Data Collected During Classroom Fieldwork

Teacher	Heather	Jasmine	Melanie	Veronica	Total
Year of teaching	3rd	4th	1st	1st	n/a
Race/Ethnicity	White	African American	Caribbean	African American	n/a
School details during period of study as defined by National Center for Education Statistics (Hoffman, 2007)	Sampler High School • Large suburban • 908 students • 4% students of color • 13% students eligible for free or reduced lunch	Alpha High School • Large suburban • 1,525 students • 40% students of color • 28% students eligible for free or reduced lunch	Young High School • Urban • 863 students • 70% students of color • 43% students eligible for free or reduced lunch	Cooper High School • Fringe rural • 257 students • 39% students of color • 21% students eligible for free or reduced lunch	n/a
Period of study	March–June 2009	January 2010	February–June 2010	February–June 2010	n/a
English class structure	Year-long, 45-minute classes	Semester-long, 90-minute classes	Semester-long, 90-minute classes	Semester-long, 90-minute classes	n/a
Fieldwork visits	13 visits to two 10th-grade classes (= 26)	5 visits to one 9th-grade class (= 5)	10 visits to two 9th-grade classes (= 20)	12 visits to two 9th-grade classes (= 24)	75
Hours of observation (hours of coded video)	16.5 (9)	7.8 (7.8)	29.5 (25.1)	34.1 (19.2)	87.9 (61.1)
Number of coded interactions	2,402	3,827	5,338	3,720	15,287
Number (percentage) of focal students	16 of 33 (48%)	9 of 21 (43%)	13 of 25 (52%)	21 of 46 (46%)	59 of 125 (47%)
Photographs	153	180	611	596	1,540
Exit interview length (pages)	2 hours (48 pages)	1.5 hours (36 pages)	1.5 hours (29 pages)	1.5 hours (36 pages)	6.5 hours (149 pages)

The potential implications for teacher education and school administration based on this finding are enormous:

- How might preservice teacher preparation programs change their course of study in order to equip new teachers to give 47% of their students special attention?
- How could in-service teacher development better assist new and experienced teachers in managing the needs of and communications with this 47%?
- How might administrators alter their assignments of new teachers either to reduce this percentage or to provide more time for such attention?

Studying Interactions and Their Contexts

During the classes I observed, I took fieldnotes and recorded video, focusing on the teachers, who graciously wore a wireless microphone. Because I believe that teacher/student interactions both before and after class time are important and warranted inclusion in the study, I began recording before the first student arrived and stopped after the last student left. I included in my analysis all interactions between the teacher and the students, and excluded interactions between students that were unrelated to the teacher. Every interaction was identified, logged in an Excel spreadsheet with a timestamp that was linked to the video, and coded for six variables:

1. The kind of class activity during which it occurred (e.g., before class, teacher-led discussion, small-group work)
2. Whether it was literacy- or social-focused
3. Whether it was initiated by teacher or student
4. The names of teacher and student(s) involved
5. Whether the student(s) involved were focal students
6. Whether the student(s) involved passed for the year (this category was added after the data collection period)

To establish context for the interactions, I gathered and analyzed artifacts (including photographs of classroom décor, the inside and outside of the school buildings, and the neighborhood communities, as well as the teachers' written feedback on students' work), kept notes on my post-observation debriefings with the teachers, and conducted exit interviews with them. The teachers also provided me with regular printed updates on their students' grades in English—on both specific assignments and the status of their overall English grade.

BOOK OVERVIEW

This book provides new ways to view interactions between teachers and students as being connected with their positioning toward retention, and it also offers practitioners ways that they can interact intentionally with students to bolster their own and their students' positioning toward retention. In focusing exclusively on teacher/student interactions, this book intends to suggest neither that improving these interactions alone will increase retention nor that improving retention ought to be a responsibility that falls solely on teachers. Instead, I seek to build on the body of research that consistently affirms the importance of belonging in retention by exploring what belonging can look like, even in the "smallest spaces"—not just for students but also for teachers, and not just to improve retention as an end in itself but also as a means to build a more equitable society.

Chapter 2 considers how classroom décor functions as an important visual interaction. I guide teachers to critically analyze their own educational spaces and intentionally create visual spaces that tether themselves and their students to one another and to their schools.

In Chapter 3, I examine spontaneous interactions in classrooms and demonstrate how they can create a pull-in or a pushout culture over time. Paying particular attention to the interactions involving students who were "falling through the cracks," I identify conversational "cracks" that these teachers and students experienced, explore how easily they can develop, and suggest ways that teachers can work to prevent or repair them.

In Chapter 4, I propose that teachers' interactions with students before and after class are critically important and worthy of special attention. I describe how, during the busy moments between classes, the teachers positioned themselves and their students toward retention in ways that are not possible during class time. I suggest strategies for teachers to use so that they can take full advantage of these key sites of possibility for interacting with their focal students.

Chapter 5 focuses on an intentional, strategic kind of teacher/student interaction in which a teacher invites an individual student to meet with her after class. The chapter demonstrates how staying-to-talk interactions offer an especially promising yet often untapped opportunity to catch students who are falling through the cracks.

In Chapter 6, I propose a new taxonomy of knowledge domains for educational practice that positions "equity and social justice knowledge" as the foundational predecessor for all other categories. This taxonomy paves the way for prioritizing teacher/student interactions as a central space in which equity education can occur. The chapter closes with specific recommendations for teacher educators seeking to promote a focus on equity in their teacher preparation programs.

In the Epilogue, the four teacher participants respond to a follow-up survey conducted several years after the original study concluded. They describe how their interactions with students and commitments to equity-oriented classroom teaching changed over time, and they give advice to new and preservice teachers about how to teach for equity as they interact with their students.

CHAPTER 2

Classroom Décor as Interaction

Teachers' Equity Orientations
Made Visible in Local Contexts

> Seeing comes before words. It is seeing which establishes our place in the surrounding world; we explain that world with words, but words can never undo the fact that we are surrounded by it. The relation between what we see and what we know is never settled. (Berger, 1984, p. 7)

Although teachers' work typically is considered to be primarily oral and written, the visual element of their work is substantial and significant. Teachers are in many regards artists, and their largest canvas—much larger than even the chalkboard, the whiteboard, or the screen on which they project their presentations—is their classroom. This chapter examines classroom décor as a visual language (Hall, Evans, & Nixon, 1997) that is interactive in multiple ways, communicates a teacher's stance on equity, and contributes to positioning toward retention.

The visual language of the classroom should be intentionally considered by teachers as an important aspect of their professional practice. First, classroom décor is a product of the interactions between teachers' beliefs and their contexts; the artifacts that teachers choose to display grow out of their experiences within the many contexts in which they have been and are situated. Second, at the same time, when teachers display artifacts, they often make visible their positioning toward one or more of these contexts. Third, items of classroom décor themselves function as interactions. They are initiated by teachers and directed toward those—students, colleagues, administrators, and even the teachers themselves—who will "read" them as visual texts.

Classroom décor functions both as process and as product and is always shifting in audience and purpose. It acts as an umbrella interaction, a meta-interaction physically and ideologically surrounding other teacher/student interactions, a visual background against which teachers' and students' oral interactions can be interpreted. Although this book focuses primarily on spoken interactions between teachers and their students, such interactions occur in physical spaces, and when teachers decorate their physical spaces, they are communicating volumes with their students before anyone says a word. Classroom décor represents one aspect of what Geneva Gay (2002) names "symbolic curriculum," which she defines as "images, symbols, icons, mottoes, awards, celebrations, and other artifacts that are used to teach students knowledge, skills, morals, and values" (p. 108).

Particular teaching contexts can draw out or necessitate particular kinds of equity-oriented approaches, and therefore there are many different ways to be an equity-oriented teacher—as many different ways as there are different contexts in which to teach. With their classroom décor, teachers can signal how they are translating their previously decontextualized, intangible beliefs into highly contextualized, tangible school spaces.

CONSIDERING LOCAL CONTEXTS, FIGURED WORLDS, ARTIFACTS, AND PIVOTING

It is a rite of passage for those of us who hope to become teachers to spend a great deal of time dreaming about what our classrooms will look like; through imagining the space we wish to create, we imagine what kind of teachers we will be. Concrete block walls painted white, maybe windows on one side, desks and chairs, bulletin boards, cabinets, a clock, and a chalkboard or whiteboard—this is the traditional classroom canvas on which teachers paint. But while its physical walls and bulletin boards may be blank upon the teacher's arrival, the classroom canvas's framing isn't blank. It is imbued with multiple contexts—the department, the hallway, the building, the school district, and even the neighborhood community in which it is physically, ideologically, and politically situated. A teacher's classroom canvas also is imbued with "school-ness," a shared set of perceptions of and associations with what we experience as "school," or more specifically for this book, "public high school." The idea of *figured worlds*, "our . . . taken for granted assumptions about what is 'typical' or 'normal'" (Gee, 2014, p. 96), is helpful here. The figured world of "school," for example, includes shared perceptions of what school spaces look, feel, and sound like, as well as the kinds of values, behaviors, and people that characterize them. In "school," visual and aural artifacts figure prominently, artifacts like hall passes, chairs attached to desks, the ringing of bells, morning announcements, lockers in long hallways, and pencil sharpeners attached to walls.

As Holland, Lachicotte, Skinner, and Cain (1998) explain, "Artifacts are *pivotal*. . . . [They] 'open up' figured worlds. They are the means by which figured worlds are evoked, collectively developed, individually learned, and made socially and personally powerful" (p. 61, emphasis in original). As these researchers note, the concept of "pivot" comes from Vygotsky's (1978) work on children's play that focused on how children use material objects "to pivot or shift into the frame of a different world.

Toys, even sticks assigned the status of horse, can be the pivots" (p. 50). Similarly, for equity-oriented teachers, ~~intentionally including pivotal items in their classroom décor can help them and their students shift out of the figured world of "school" and into one centered on issues of social justice.~~

When new, equity-oriented teachers arrive in a classroom, faced with the prospect of making it their own, they must often decide how consistent their classroom space is going to be with the local contexts and with the figured world of "school," and how much risk they are going to take in featuring décor that represents an equity orientation. For these new teachers, then, decisions about classroom décor represent some of their first major pedagogical choices and carry significant personal and political weight. When new, equity-oriented teachers make decisions about classroom décor, they intentionally and visually orient themselves with and/or against the grain of what counts as typical "school" décor in their local contexts.

Among the chosen items of décor in any classroom, a visual dialogue occurs between the discourses of "school"-ness and alternative figured worlds. While some items seem intended primarily for students, others for the teacher, and still others for "snoopervisors" (Wiles & Bondi, 1980), teachers typically do not make the purpose of classroom décor items explicit. Instead, they are teacher-initiated interactions that, every moment, communicate messages to classroom visitors in silence.

For many marginalized or minoritized people, unfortunately, the figured world of "school" often is associated with pushout culture, as described in Chapter 1, and equity-oriented teachers must understand that in whatever context they find themselves, an equity orientation will always be in tension with pushout culture. Although this book focuses on teachers' language and use of their power to interact humanely with their students, teachers work against large systemic oppressions that often result in both teachers' and students' dehumanization. Training teachers to identify and critically investigate visual pushout culture may be

> **Pivotal classroom objects for equity-oriented teachers:**
> - Are visual reminders of their equity commitments
> - Can trigger a mental shift in the teacher

one strategy to help root it out and to replace it with visual pull-in or retention culture. Classroom décor typically is not addressed in teacher preparation or professional development, yet I urge teachers to consider the messages that their visual texts may be sending to both their students and themselves. In the remainder of this chapter, I examine how equity-oriented teachers use their classroom décor strategically in the context of their local communities to create the humanizing, hopeful, and/or challenging spaces that their students need.

USING PERSONAL ITEMS AS
PIVOTAL VISUAL ANCHORS IN LOCAL CONTEXTS

In a classroom constantly swirling with activity, equity-oriented teachers use personal items in their classroom décor as a visual anchor for their core beliefs, particularly as those items appear most relevant to their local context. These visual anchors can work as Vygotskian pivots that help teachers look beyond the pervasive figured world of "school" evoked by their physical surroundings and "shift into" an equity-focused state of mind in which they imagine and remember to work toward what is possible: a more equitable, empowered future for youth. Such pivotal artifacts can help counteract pushout culture on two levels: They help teachers recall their core beliefs, stay inspired, and thus work in small ways against teacher pushout culture; and when teachers can focus on matters of equity, they can help create a pull-in culture for students.

Teachers often include pivotal décor on the wall space behind and around their desks, and on their desks themselves. As teachers' desk areas can function as a place of relative respite for teachers in their busy classrooms, the primary audience for pivotal objects situated there is most often the teachers rather than the students, and these items can provide some intellectual, physical, or spiritual comfort to teachers when they are able to sit down at their desks. Another key area where teachers display pivotal artifacts is on their classroom doors, particularly the inside of the doors. These are noteworthy surfaces because everyone entering or leaving the classroom passes them in close proximity, and because they are highly visible, both from the hallway when the door is open and from the inside of the classroom, whether the door is open or closed.

Because of classroom décor's primarily silent communication, in my research I chose not to ask the four teacher participants about their décor. Instead, I write about it in the following sections from the perspective of an inquisitive classroom visitor without special knowledge of the agentive teacher's decisionmaking behind each item.

Heather

Heather Fredrick's school is located in a small, working-class town comprising two White communities with a somewhat contentious history. One part of the community, in which the school is located, was established earlier and has the feel of small-town America, with tree-lined streets and grassy yards surrounding one-story detached houses. The second part, developed later as part of a wartime industry, has the austere structure and feel of military barracks and included, at least during the time I spent there, many vacant commercial properties. Over decades, the first community variously sought to distance itself from the second, but in the end, youth from both communities attend the same high school, as no other public high school options are available for community residents. The grafted-in historical context of the school is evident in a majestic original stone building with Ionic columns—next to which stand brick-fronted additions constructed in response to the widening population the school serves. These contexts seemed to linger in the students' social segregation, aided structurally by the school's use of tracking students into general, college-prep, and honors/ AP classes (Oakes, 1985). Entering Heather's classroom felt a lot like entering a late 1960s or early 1970s time capsule—orange wall-to-wall carpeting and a wood-paneled wall dominated the space in spite of Heather's best efforts. The orange carpet and wood paneling seemed to issue silent challenges to the mere idea of change, illuminating for me the great significance and deep-seated nature of our teaching contexts, the long histories that new, equity-oriented teachers enter.

A 3rd-year teacher in this context, Heather experienced a great deal of fear caused by four main factors: her untenured status, a downsizing district climate in which it was either explicitly communicated or heavily implied that several untenured teachers would be let go at year's end, an administrator with a big personality with whom Heather had clashed, and the sometimes-difficult nature of a small-town context. As Heather reflected in an end-of-year interview:

> I don't want to make too many waves, and I think with the way that town works . . . I feel like I have a pretty decent reputation right now, and I don't want to ever chip away at that just because it's a small town, and everybody talks, and you get one bad thing, then foosh! No joke, there it is.

Behind Heather's desk was a bulletin board on which she had pinned many pivotal items. Four objects were the largest and thus most noticeable:

- A poster in bright pastel colors featuring a quote attributed to Einstein: "You have to color outside the lines once in a while if you want to make your life a masterpiece"
- The front of a greeting card with the words: "Be the change you wish to see in the world"
- A poster of Picasso's *Don Quixote*
- An original pastel featuring blues and greens and a tree's reflection in a body of water

That two of these artifacts issue challenges to the viewer ("You have to color outside the lines . . ." and "Be the change . . .") seems significant: Because Heather placed these pivotal objects behind her desk, she may have sought to remind or challenge herself to work against the status quo. To me, the combined effect of these quotations, the beautiful pastel colors and artwork, the Picasso/Cervantes image concerned with the nature of reality, and the homage to a quixotic journey, is one in which truth and fiction—and serenity and restlessness—are being held in tension. In my reading, the tension among these images provides a compelling visual demonstration of Heather's positionality as a White equity-oriented teacher in a mostly White community. Her choice of classroom décor, which could be seen as subtly, rather than overtly, communicating her social justice orientation, was a byproduct of the way she read the local contexts in which she was enmeshed; she seemed to choose visual rhetoric that would not automatically alienate visitors to her classroom but rather, perhaps, ensure that they would stay long enough to engage in conversations toward meaningful change. Heather's filling of her classroom with so many personal, pivotal items may signal her investment in the space and a positive positioning toward retention.

Jasmine

Jasmine Brown's school stands on the outskirts of an urban center amid a tangle of industrial railroad tracks, major highways, power lines, transmission towers, and telephone poles. Chain-link fences surround Alpha High School, an intimidatingly large, dark, old school that looks from the outside like a brick fortress, with few windows and no landscaping or art. Alpha was officially classified by the National Center for Education Statistics as being in a "large suburban" community (Hoffman, 2007), and over the past 20 years, the inner suburbs have seen a decrease in education and income levels (Juday, 2015; Renn, 2014).

Jasmine chose to teach at Alpha because she wanted to "go where . . . the need is" and saw similarities between Alpha students and herself as a young person. She saw Alpha as more supportive of diversity than were the urban schools where she had been a student. During a NETS meeting she attended as a 2nd-year teacher, she explained that she saw, "as a teenager, . . . how certain teachers were targeted and eliminated because they were trying to do more for their students than the administrators thought was appropriate for these kids who, they feel, really aren't worth the trouble." An African American woman who persevered through a difficult upbringing, as a teacher Jasmine cultivated an equity orientation centered on uplifting young people facing similar difficulties:

> My initial reason for going into teaching was to reach the students who usually couldn't be reached, since, for the majority of the teachers in the school system, there is no connection. The teachers haven't really experienced anything that really set them back. These kids have, so it's

hard to relate. If your life has been easy and has been laid out for you, you can't relate to the kid whose parents are on drugs or who's being abused at home on a regular basis.

Intentionally placing herself into this context as a new teacher who sought to foster a different, more connected kind of teacher/student relationship was one of Jasmine's first equity-oriented moves as a teacher: She sought to understand, celebrate, comfort, advise, and serve students as a model of a smart, strong, proud Black woman in a context where students otherwise felt second-class.

As a new teacher, Jasmine felt excluded by other teachers for being a student advocate, but persevered in her positive work with students and families so that, by the end of her third and final untenured year, she had cultivated a track record in the community that, she believed, served to protect her. Jasmine's experiences of being excluded by her colleagues, unfortunately, did not end when she earned tenure, which had just occurred when I spent time in her classroom for this study. At this point in her career, she believed that she and Alpha were a good match in the sense that there she was able to be the kind of teacher she wanted to be. Yet she had experienced unfriendliness from multiple people and in numerous ways, particularly through being overtly and covertly ignored or excluded or being verbally intimidated—microaggressive strategies commonly used to minoritize people (Sellers & Shelton, 2003; Solórzano, Ceja, & Yosso, 2000) and instill in them a sense that they are a Nobody (Hill, 2016). Such actions are part and parcel of pushout culture, which can push out teachers just as much as students.

On the inside of her classroom door, Jasmine placed a poster entitled "Determination/Little Rock Nine," which featured large photographs of the nine Black students who integrated Central High School in Little Rock, Arkansas, in 1957. Below the photos are the words, "The size of the obstacle is unimportant; having the courage and conviction to overcome it is important." The poster's large size and bold white-on-black colors dominated the four worn, taped-together printouts of course objectives in tiny font that Jasmine had taped next to it (see Figure 2.1). The visual juxtaposition seems to illustrate quite dramatically the difference between Jasmine's valuing of the given curriculum and her own. In fact, the Little Rock Nine poster seems to render the course objectives marginal or even insignificant by comparison.

Jasmine created in her classroom a visual world that prominently featured and celebrated the identities and stories of two groups of people: her students and famous inspirational members of the Black community. Around her desk, she placed dozens of her former students' graduation pictures and memorabilia like photographs of her own children and other loved ones. On the far wall, she posted her students' drawings of their names and favorite things, and under the whiteboard, she displayed an illustrated "Key

Figure 2.1. Jasmine's Door and Little Rock Nine Poster

Moments in African American History." In a school where Jasmine experienced profound isolation from her colleagues and administrators, she created a classroom space in which she and all the students who visited her were surrounded at all times by images of her people—pivotal visual artifacts that could serve as reminders of enduring connections; as reasons to be proud of themselves, past, present, and future; and as incentives to stay in school and reach their goals.

Veronica

The newness of Cooper High School, where Veronica James taught, engendered a feeling of promise that was magnified by its environs, with seemingly endless fields and waterways visited twice a year by thousands of migrating snow geese. It seemed that change appeared both literally and figuratively on the horizon. After Cooper opened in this area, which was transitioning from rural to suburban, the planting of developers' conquering flags gradually replaced the planting of farmers' crops in the fields. Although the roads in the region generally were bumpy, narrow, and unlined, the one leading to Cooper abruptly became paved and lined about a quarter mile from the school. Bulldozers and dump trucks signaled to visitors of Cooper High School, even before they caught a glimpse of the school, that change was coming. Cooper High School itself was a sight to behold. In the new, clean hallways, the brightness of the overhead lights reflected everywhere, off the gleaming floors and the sparkling lockers. Its location befitting the vast (for now) farmland, the sprawling building featured wide, open spaces—including a two-story atrium that seemed to boast of how much space its designers could afford to waste.

For Veronica, job insecurity was almost nonexistent; as she quipped at the end of the year, "It's a brand-new school; how are they going to get rid of teachers?" Although the staff at Cooper High School consisted of primarily new teachers, Veronica characterized them positively as "tight-knit" with open minds. Especially for 1st-year teachers, this kind of alignment, security, and camaraderie is rare. Veronica seemed to have arrived at this sense of satisfaction after the first few months of teaching, during which she experienced the common stresses of planning short-term and long-term curriculum for multiple classes for the first time. But she also seemed to have arrived at this sense of satisfaction by "stay[ing] out of district stuff" and "not eating lunch with other teachers," the former out of a desire to avoid the "political"—"I just want to teach the babies"—and the latter because "I love my co-workers . . . [and] like my style of teaching; I don't want to be influenced to be mean."

Two small pivotal items, books, were displayed on Veronica's front windowsill. Standing up vertically, they appeared between potted plants, their covers facing the classroom. Placed away from the main traffic flows of the classroom, they likely were seen only by the few students with seats close to this window or by students visiting Veronica's desk. One cover featured the word PEACE, and the other, DREAM. Upon closer inspection, it is clear that the books included photographs and writings of Rev. Dr. Martin Luther King, Jr., whom Veronica named a hero in her exit interview. These two small books were the only personal items I observed in Veronica's classroom, a smallness I read as consistent with her strong focus on helping students achieve success in meeting goals, a focus that may have caused her to regard any display of her own personality, history, or interests in her classroom as irrelevant. Instead, she saw her classroom primarily as a tool that could contribute to student success.

Melanie

Like the knot or line that marks the center of a tug-of-war rope, Young High School stands not only between a city's financial center and one of its most impoverished neighborhoods, but also between its traditional neighborhood schools and charter schools. The building itself even houses both a historic section and a more contemporary section. At one point during my research, members of the Young community found themselves the near-constant topic of city and state headlines. Assigned the lowest "school ranking" and placed on "academic watch" status for continued low student test scores, Young stood at the center of a media maelstrom as politicians, educational reformers, educators, and community members tugged it back and forth, debating what was going wrong and what should be done. Persistent rumors swirled about a possible closing or takeover in which the majority of teachers and administrators would be fired, fostering tangible fear in the Young community. Inside the school, a takeover of sorts had already begun, both with many experienced teachers retiring or changing schools to avoid the unpleasant changes they saw on Young's horizon and with many new teachers taking their places.

As a 1st-year teacher, Melanie entered Young when it was scrambling to find its footing, with a host of young staff assuming new administrative posts and a host of even younger staff, like her, assuming new teaching positions. Like other urban teachers in schools enduring high teacher turnover, Melanie seemed to come up empty everywhere she looked for support. A Caribbean female teaching in a school with few teachers of color—and even fewer, if any, new teachers of color—Melanie, like Jasmine and Veronica, shouldered the weight of racial/ethnic under-representation atop the weight of newness to the profession. Although she admired how well the Young administrators and experienced teachers knew, interacted with, and supported the students, she did not experience the same supportive treatment. Instead, for example, Melanie watched during a meeting as an experienced teacher claimed that he was too busy and exhausted to meet any of the new teachers; as her greetings to other teachers she passed in the hallway went unreturned; and as her colleagues increasingly took sides in personal "drama" and tried to pull her into the equation. Trying to remain neutral, appear cheerful, and be supportive of everyone else was difficult, and by the end of her first year, she confided that there weren't too many people she could talk to, and she still didn't know whom to trust—a lack of connection that can quickly wither a teacher's positioning toward retention.

Administrators at Young missed many opportunities to support Melanie; these oversights added up to create uncertainty and stress, unnecessarily contributing to an already-present pushout culture that is toxic for new teachers and particularly toxic for new teachers in under-resourced schools. One such missed opportunity occurred in Melanie's second month of teaching when her keys, money, and credit cards were stolen by some of her female students. Although she immediately reported the incident to the school's disciplinarian and then to the principal, they did not help her. NETS teachers, including Jasmine, shared Melanie's sense of helplessness during one of our meetings, wondering how to proceed when Young administrators' lack of response may have stemmed from worries that the more disciplinary incidents they placed on record, the more negative press and the fewer students and funding they would receive.

I witnessed other examples of administrator-imposed stress: Melanie and her colleagues had to begin first period without knowing when it would be cut short for a planned assembly; a major school announcement to which students obviously were going to have strong reactions was made during first period when it could have been saved until the end of the day; and two of the four 9th graders placed on Young's no-pass list during the first semester were assigned to the same English class, a second-semester class taught by Melanie, a 1st-year teacher. The isolation Melanie felt from her colleagues and administrators was compounded by a remote location: Her classroom was a small, windowless basement room, far away from any other academic classroom.

Just inside the door of her classroom and thus equally visible to herself and to her students, Melanie had hung a significant pivotal item, a "Quote Wall" on red poster board, the only handwritten item displayed in the room (see Figure 2.2). Each of the four pivotal quotes she included exhibited a firm, determined hopefulness in individual potential that is possible to reach once negative circumstances, people, or mindsets are overcome—an important message for both Melanie and her students.

CREATING VISUAL EQUITY-ORIENTED CURRICULUM IN THE ABSENCE OF PUSHOUT CULTURE

In addition to displaying personal items that serve as visual anchors for their commitments, equity-oriented teachers can use classroom décor to amplify aspects of their subject matter that are uniquely suited to the social justice needs they see in their local context.

Heather's work at Sampler High School provides an important example for equity-oriented teachers who work in schools that are not entrenched in pushout culture. At schools like Sampler, where almost all of the students and teachers are White, new, and equity-oriented, teachers can use their classroom décor to foster students' sense of empathy and interconnectedness among people from diverse backgrounds.

Heather

During one discussion we had about differing approaches to social justice education, Heather explained her hesitancy to embrace Darling-Hammond, French, and Garcia-Lopez's (2002) belief that teachers should lead students in explicitly examining inequities in their communities and promoting more equitable paths forward. Instead, in her own context, Heather felt that the best way to maintain her ability to effect change was to ensure her job

Figure 2.2. Melanie's Pivotal Quote Wall

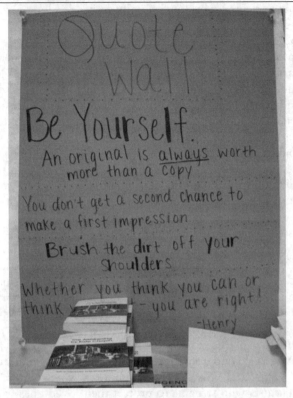

security by avoiding doing anything that might attract the attention of an administrator or anyone in the town:

> These productive dialogues, I think they have to be stealthfully done, 'cause if you say, "Now look at how unfair this is," it kind of turns them off. People here don't want to talk about stuff that's uncomfortable, so you can kind of sneak it in and embed it in a greater idea. Like, okay, so you've got a crab, right, on the beach: If you go grab for that crab from the front, it's out of here, it's gone. But if you grab the crab from the back, you can hold onto it and make it have that conversation, which is how I feel like I have had to approach a lot of this. Like, okay, these people are coming from different situations, or somebody who's really, you know, kind of hard up in his life. I feel like some of the issues are very touchy with them especially in this town because you've got [the two different communities].

Heather's classroom décor choices, whether consciously or not, seem to narrate the story of an equity-oriented teacher "grabbing the crab from the back," a compelling metaphor for her intentional process of engaging in subtle change-oriented work at this point in her teaching career and in her local contexts.

The largest and most prominent pieces of décor in Heather's classroom were the posters of film adaptations of some of the texts her classes were reading, particularly *A Doll's House* and *Antigone* (see Figure 2.3), and three student-made collages evoking Big Brother, which were taped onto a row of cabinets and surrounded a *1984* movie poster. To the casual observer, these objects seemed to support a dominant narrative, celebrating the traditional literary canon and noting its presence even in popular media; further, the bodies depicted in these prominent images were White, like those of all of the students and teachers I observed in the room. However, a subtle connection among the three texts prominently featured in Heather's room is that all center protagonists who question injustice and endure difficult consequences when they defy the status quo and act toward what they believe is right.

Consistent with Heather's subtle approach, the change-oriented artifacts in Heather's classroom were far from its largest or most obvious décor; in fact, their equity orientation may not even have been apparent to her students, at least not immediately. First, on the classroom wall space that most often functions as prime real estate—the area above the primary chalkboard or whiteboard—Heather placed a row of novels, partially visible in Figure 2.3. On a section of the wall space to the left of that shown in the photograph, Heather placed novels that were absent from the curriculum she was teaching. In this notably more diverse selection of literature, Achebe's *Things Fall Apart* and Wilson's *Fences*—both of which feature strong Black male protagonists who struggle to protect their loved ones from harm in a racist world—were highlighted most prominently beneath the classroom's only clock, a high-visibility location. To my knowledge, Heather did not call explicit attention to her inclusion of these diverse works of literature in her classroom space in spite of their exclusion from her required curriculum; instead, the novels were wordlessly given visual distinction and could serve as the background against which the students viewed their teacher each day. Similar in theme but out of students' usual lines of sight, a collage featuring postcards from across the globe was posted on the wall toward the back of the room. This collage, comprising images from across the United States and of Tokyo, Singapore, Paris, Mexico, and Australia, for example, served as a silent reminder to Heather's students that the world was much bigger than what they currently were seeing and experiencing.

CREATING A VISUAL RESPITE FROM PUSHOUT CULTURE

In contrast to Heather's context at Sampler, numerous visual artifacts of pushout, of policing, appeared in the three other schools—Jasmine's, Melanie's, and Veronica's. Importantly, and sadly, these artifacts appeared

Figure 2.3. Subtle Change-Oriented Artifacts in Heather's Classroom

in direct correlation with each school's poverty data, which were also in direct correlation with each school's population of students of color (refer to Table 1.1). Two examples of the hiding-in-plain-sight pushout curriculum of classroom décor can serve to illustrate this trend. First, the more seemingly innocuous: While I saw no hallway/bathroom passes at Sampler High School (4% students of color; 13% of students eligible for free/reduced lunch), required bathroom passes contributed significantly to classroom décor and life at the three other high schools (39–70% students of color; 21–43% of students eligible for free/reduced lunch). At Young High School, Melanie's school, where these numbers were highest, some students ("on special passes" or "on the no-pass list") were required to be accompanied on during-class excursions by a disciplinarian, which meant that the teacher had to phone the office any time particular students needed to go to the bathroom, the library, or their locker—a requirement that made not only the physical passes, but phone calls to the office and the presence of disciplinarians, regular visual pushout features of Young classroom life. Second and less seemingly innocuous, the same kind of correlation occurred with respect to the number and gravity of official documents posted in the classroom. At Alpha, Cooper, and Young, I observed school uniform regulations, discipline policies, evacuation plans, and, perhaps most terrifying, a laminated "Homeland Security Threat Level Action Plan." Only at Sampler, the school with few students in poverty and few students of color, did I observe no such official documents posted in the classroom. While posting of disaster preparedness materials may have been mandatory and/or initially may not seem indicative of pushout culture, it is deeply disturbing that such visual artifacts appeared only in schools with high numbers of students of color and students in poverty.

Inseparable from the reality that pushout culture pervaded Alpha, Cooper, and Young High Schools is the reality that Jasmine, Melanie, and Veronica are all teachers of color. Although the American teaching profession as a whole remains disproportionately White (U.S. Department of Education, 2016), teachers of color are likelier than White teachers to teach in schools that serve primarily students of color and students in poverty (Achinstein, Ogawa, Sexton, & Freitas, 2010). The need to increase the retention of teachers of color is well documented (e.g., Sleeter, Neal, & Kumashiro, 2015) and provides one important way to enrich the education of students in under-resourced schools. Jasmine, Melanie, and Veronica provide important insights into how equity-oriented teachers of color in schools entrenched in pushout culture can use their classroom décor to create a visual respite that elevates student knowledge, voices, and pride.

> Equity-oriented teachers in schools entrenched in push-out culture can use their classroom décor to create a visual respite that elevates student knowledge, voices, and pride.

Jasmine

Through her classroom décor, Jasmine encouraged her students to meet their goals and thrive. This message emanated primarily from the artifacts featured on the main wall of her classroom, as shown in Figure 2.4. The focal point of Jasmine's room, the largest feature of her décor, was the banner "Attitude is the mind's paintbrush. It can color any situation," stretched above the expanse of two chalkboards. Consistent with Jasmine's positive approach to student motivation, the banner contained the kind of gentle challenge that she tends toward in her teaching. The sign's message places squarely on the students responsibility for—and establishes an expectation of—having a good attitude, but does so in a beautiful, kind, persuasive way. This pushing of students toward self-determination and self-efficacy is consistent with an equity orientation, as it increases the agency of people who have been historically vulnerable and subject to others' intentions for them rather than determining their own intentions and being able to actualize them.

Perhaps the most important feature of Jasmine's classroom décor, one through which she invited herself and her students to share their experiences, was the poetry wall that appears on the right side of Figure 2.4, underneath the American flag and a poster depicting serene waters with the words, "Everyone has a story to tell." Jasmine's poetry wall featured

Figure 2.4. Jasmine's Focal Banner and Poetry Wall

student poetry: Anyone who wanted to post a poem there could do so, and they could either include their name or post their work anonymously. During my visits, the poetry wall contained 10–15 student poems, titled, for example, "The Girl Who Drank a Lot," "Mii MuNdOo" ["Myy WoRlDd"], "Paradise and Tranquility," "I Am From," and "A Reflection of an Individual." Like the pivotal artifacts around Heather's desk, Jasmine's pivotal poetry wall, which included several of her own poems, stood next to her desk.

The poetry wall, like so many other aspects of Jasmine's classroom décor, appeared to be an emancipatory, revolutionary, equity-oriented teaching move, a seed that grew out of her own identity, took root, and grew in the hostile ground of Alpha High School. In her exit interview, Jasmine reminded me how important it is to understand that teacher/student interactions are a drop in the bucket of all of the interactions that students have, and that any understanding of teacher/student interactions has to take those other interactions into consideration. For example, if students are being abused by an authority figure, or an adult has failed to protect them in some way, Jasmine explained, "They don't trust anything, anything that they see: school, nothing." For this reason, and in this context, Jasmine crafted an approach to interact particularly with her most vulnerable students, an approach without which, she believed, her attempts likely would go unheard:

> It's really hard to get them to focus on their academics when everything else is so powerful and negative in their lives that they don't see that as

being helpful. It's hard to understand that English is helpful when you live with a child molester because that's not going to help you with that. If it's not going to help you get out of that situation, then it's not helpful. And so I focus on saying, "Okay, English is this class with skills you're going to learn for college and the next years." I focus on, "Writing is a form of expression for you to get things out, and the more you write, the better you'll feel. You get it out."

Jasmine's contrast between "English class" as an entity that is temporary in time and space and "writing" as having more enduring time and purpose seemed to be mirrored in her classroom décor, which clearly privileged "writing" over "English."

The poetry wall also appeared to be a place in and from which Jasmine could serve as a role model for her students in ways that go beyond the traditional curriculum, at considerable personal risk to her. Jasmine noted that when she became a newly tenured teacher, she began to share more of her personal stories of survival with her students than she had shared when she was untenured, but that she felt that taking this risk, both then and now, was compulsory:

I had to start sharing my poems and my own personal stories so that they saw that [whatever struggle they currently were experiencing] is not going to define who they are for the rest of their lives. [But] a teacher warned me . . . , "You shouldn't share. If [students] go home and tell their parent, and the parent calls and makes a big deal, you're going to get in trouble." That's possible, but that kid wasn't going to start trying if I didn't. There's no long-term view [for teenagers]. You can barely see next year! You think, "I'm 14 or 15. I'm hurting. I'm depressed. I'm cutting myself, and I have to hide it. I'm drinking. And I don't see any way out. I *do* see the people who are living on the streets, on the corner, the prostitutes, people that wind up in prison or are dead. I *don't* know about the people who went through this and are okay now." So I had to share. I wrote a poem second semester, and I read it for the creative writing slam, for the students and teachers to know that I am putting myself out here on purpose. This is not an accident. . . .The kids have to see that they'll be okay.

It is important to note that Jasmine's empathy and poetry wall weren't ends in themselves but rather means, used by an equity-oriented teacher, to other ends: ensuring that the vulnerable youth in her classroom felt seen, valued, and encouraged to persevere. The messages of the poetry wall in her room, particularly of her own poetry, seemed to be designed to endure long after her poetry lessons and poetry slam concluded, reminding her students that "they'll be okay." The poetry wall worked together with the other items of décor on this focal wall to attempt to facilitate what hooks (1994) names "coming to voice," in which people share their experiences, not just as an end in and of itself, but in order to become emboldened to speak out more broadly. Through this piece of her classroom décor, Jasmine's own voice and the voices of her students could join together to share encouragement to survive, stay in school together, and thrive.

Melanie

Melanie took a positive but minimalist approach to classroom décor. Whether this approach stemmed from the busyness of being a new teacher, a lack of funds, Young's aforementioned reputation and some history of theft within its walls, a combination of these, or none of these, it suggested a tentative positioning toward retention. Its sparseness was reminiscent of a room or apartment being rented for only a short time, the occupant perhaps unwittingly establishing no enduring connection with the space. Perhaps, though, the relatively few but hopeful artifacts of décor in Melanie's room heighten their importance, given that each item is made obvious and highly visible in the space.

On the bulletin board closest to Melanie's desk, contrasting images seemed to illustrate the kind of "dialectic struggle" that Greene (1995) saw between a painter and the canvas. The left half of the bulletin board featured a multitude of 8½" x 11" "school-ness" artifacts with titles like "Classroom Expectations," "Uniform Policy Examples," and "District Attendance Policy." One seemingly positive but overly deterministic (and, for students who are struggling academically, fairly terrifying) paper on this bulletin board, as shown in Figure 2.5, was titled "What's Your Path?" and featured flowcharts of steps that apparently lead toward four outcomes: "Go to a 4-year college," "Go to a 2-year college or apprentice program," "Go to work or enter military," or "Be a bum." The flowchart for this fourth outcome began with "Fail courses," a powerful, upsetting artifact of pushout culture.

Next to these items, near the center of this bulletin board, appeared a small yellow poster board onto which Melanie had taped a few personal, pivotal objects, creating a collage-like ensemble. These objects included photocopies of her degrees, three photographs of Melanie with loved ones, a small professional football insignia, and a concert ticket and photograph. To the right of this poster board was tacked a month-by-month calendar. It seemed as if Melanie was sticking a cautious toe into the water of sharing herself with her students, using artifacts that emphasized her professional preparation, revealed that she was a football and music fan, and demonstrated enviable fashion in photos with smiling friends and family. These pivotal personal artifacts offer images of human dignity, of enjoyment in sports and the arts, of family and friends, images that contrast with those on the left side of the board. But visually, while Melanie's yellow poster provided the only large splash of bright color and

Figure 2.5. Pushout Culture Visualized: "Be a Bum"

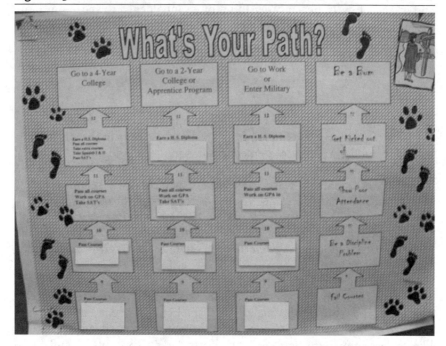

joy on this side of the room, it was overwhelmed in size and space by the predominant artifacts of "school," suggesting that "school" may have been temporarily winning this struggle. However, the right third of the bulletin board was blank, conjuring up notions of an unfinished present or an unwritten future.

Veronica

Perhaps because of the building's newness, few decorations hung on Cooper High School's walls during the time I spent there, with three exceptions. The first consisted of posters listing the names of students who had earned honor roll status for the marking period, a fairly common sight in well-funded public schools. Second, school data appeared prominently, in the form of percentages of students meeting either aspects of a schoolwide writing rubric (and their change over the marking periods) or specific standardized testing goals that administrators seemed to have set for students.

Finally, in the weeks leading up to the school's primary standardized test, 10–20 huge test-oriented posters gradually appeared in the main lobbies' hallways, visually orienting the school toward the test and increasingly emphasizing its importance. Some handwritten posters appeared to have been made by students and featured hints (such as "Remember to eat a good breakfast!") or motivational words, like "We have a job to do. . . Cream the [test]! Do Your Best." The use of the word *job* in this sign can imply that doing well on the standardized test was required—or that doing so was the primary purpose or role of youth attending this school. Other posters informed students about test pep rallies and spirit days ("Don't Sweat the Test! Wear Sweats on Monday!") leading up to the test. Some posters seemed to have been made by staff on professional large-format printers; these featured numerous references to the school data goals and AYP (adequate yearly progress) as well as images of Cooper High School faculty with inspirational or humorous speech balloons filled with messages such as "Cooper does not fear the [test]; the [test] fears us." Together, these items of décor seemed to create a visual culture that primarily valued performance measurement.

Veronica's classroom décor differed from the school's in significant ways, the most obvious of which was its prominent featuring of individual student work. By far the most notable characteristic of Veronica's classroom was the abundance of student work taped to its walls: I'd estimate that 100–150 pieces of student work created a tapestry around the room and that these items constituted about 95% of the classroom's total décor. All of the students' work featured a colorful combination of images and written text, creating a lively effect in the room. In their work posted on Veronica's classroom walls, students

- Visualized and defined the difference between commonly confused words (such as *there/they're/their, farther/further,* and *its/it's*)
- Visualized and defined word roots (such as *anti-, biblio-, geo-, mal-, mort-,* and *philo-*)
- Drew attention to worn-out words (such as *a lot, good, great, many, said, think,* and *very*)
- Presented examples of good diction (such as *gigantic, glamorous, naughty, omen,* and *superficial*), as shown in Figure 2.6.

About 15 pieces of signed student artwork also appeared behind Veronica's desk and featured subjects from SpongeBob and Slash to aliens and skateboarders.

The display of student artwork and written work made students' skills, passions, and personalities the unmistakable focus of the room. These artifacts also provided a welcome relief from the nameless, faceless, lifeless numeric data that appeared in the hallways outside each classroom. When Veronica posted the work of her students, she provided them with an audience beyond the teacher and allowed them to teach and learn from one another, even across her different classes. By valuing and visually centering student knowledge and positioning students as teachers, Veronica demonstrated powerful ways to express an equity orientation in a school focused on testing.

Figure 2.6. Veronica's Students' Diction Wall

CONCLUSION: ENACTING EQUITY-ORIENTED TEACHING WITH STRATEGIC CLASSROOM DÉCOR

As this chapter illustrates, the classroom décor of new teachers with social justice commitments can mirror and/or contrast with the larger school and community contexts in which the teachers and their students are situated. Various aspects of an equity orientation (refer to Figure 1.1) are amplified as teachers interact with/in these contexts. And when teachers engage in creating classroom décor, they initiate an important kind of interaction with their students that can both reveal and create positionings toward retention. Each teacher's physical space can serve as a metaphor, as an observable "visual language" (Hall et al., 1997) that can narrate important aspects of the teacher's lived experiences and commitments as a social justice educator. Like other forms of pedagogy, designing a classroom space affords new, equity-oriented teachers the opportunity to enact their commitments strategically in accordance with both the unique needs they perceive among their students and the level of risk they feel able to take in their unique professional contexts. For example, Heather propped up diverse books—books she was not teaching—above her chalkboard; Heather and Veronica featured student work on their classroom walls; and Jasmine celebrated Black culture in her décor and co-created a poetry wall with her students. Below, I offer teachers recommendations for overcoming obstacles in various contexts in order to engage in a critical visual analysis of their own educational spaces and learn to practice equity-oriented teaching through their classroom décor.

Obstacle #1: Not Having Space, Time, and/or Funds for Décor

Even when new, equity-oriented teachers do not yet have their own classroom assignment or do have a classroom but neither the time nor funds to invest in decorating it, they can and should still be involved in actively engaging in the design of the visual spaces in which they teach. While it would be easy, especially for new teachers, to deem décor as less instructionally important and therefore less worthy of their limited time or money, this chapter argues for the importance of décor, particularly insofar as it can both send powerful messages all year and set the stage for all future teacher/student interactions in the space. For new teachers looking to overcome these obstacles, I recommend the following:

- If you don't yet have a permanent classroom, ask the teachers in whose rooms you're teaching if they would be willing to set aside a particular area of the room—a bulletin board, a wall, or at least a portion of one—for your use. In some schools, this kind of space-sharing is standard practice, but in others, it isn't. Regardless, most experienced teachers will be sympathetic to your plight, particularly if you ask them well in advance.
- If you have a cart that you use to travel from room to room, consider how you might outfit it in ways that will help you pivot toward your equity orientation and increase your and/or your students' positioning toward retention.
- If you do have a permanent classroom assignment but are short on time or funds, collaborate and be creative. Ask your colleagues, including the librarian and art teacher, whether they have extra materials that you can use. Visit yard sales or consignment shops with your classroom in mind. Best of all, ask your students to bring in or create décor that they find inspiring and that can be integrated with your curriculum.

Obstacle #2: Fearing Getting Fired

For many new, equity-oriented teachers, the joy of getting hired is replaced relatively quickly by the fear of getting fired. Sometimes student teaching or other field experiences lacking an equity orientation can contribute to new teachers' fear; such experiences can act as an extension of the K–12 apprenticeship of observation (Lortie, 1975) and can threaten to socialize new teachers into maintaining the status quo rather than working to root inequities from the system. While of course such fear can play a role in all aspects of their practice, I suggest that new teachers take the time to focus on their classroom décor so that they see the possible manifestations of fear more clearly and thus gain more control over it. If you are a new teacher who is afraid to make your equity orientation visually observable in your classroom space, I suggest that to overcome this fear, you do the following:

- Acknowledge and inventory your fears in your particular contexts. Consider to what extent each of your teaching contexts—your community, your district, your building, and your department—is supportive of an equity orientation and how you know this. If you are not sure, train yourself to observe your visual surroundings and engage in the kinds of analysis illustrated in this chapter. Carefully identify for yourself the specific aspects of your contexts that elicit job insecurity for you, as naming fears can help spur bravery.
- Respond to your fears with carefully planned décor. Once you have identified the origins of your fears, you can determine how much of an equity orientation you plan to reveal, are already revealing, or need to dial back in your room's décor in order to obtain a healthy balance between your commitments and your job security. For example, perhaps, like Jasmine, you could create a poetry wall for your students but wait until after you are tenured to post your own poetry there.

Obstacle #3: Experiencing a Sense of Isolation

Many different contextual factors can cause equity-oriented teachers to feel that although they constantly are surrounded by people in their job, they are alone in their work. Possible isolating factors referenced in this chapter are unsupportive administrators; small-town familiarity; critical, competitive, dramatic, or malicious colleagues; a culture of despair; and overemphasis on standardized test scores. If you are a teacher who feels isolated in any of these ways, I suggest that in your classroom décor, you do the following:

- Prioritize including pivotal artifacts that remind you to build your work on the foundation of love, face your fears, and bravely maintain your commitment to working with your students toward a more equitable world. Surrounding yourself with inspiring images of and words from your equity community can remind you that you are, in fact, not alone in your work.
- Include positive, beautiful, encouraging words, images, and artifacts in your décor that can help create a pull-in culture

for both you and your students. Consider that any feelings of isolation you may be experiencing as a teacher might signal the presence of pushout culture at your school—a culture that often affects both teachers and students.

QUESTIONS FOR TEACHER REFLECTION, DISCUSSION, AND ACTION

1. What artifacts currently constitute your classroom décor? Draw a diagram or make a list of them.

2. What messages do you want to send, and to whom, with your classroom décor? What artifacts could you (re)move or add to your current décor to achieve these messages, particularly in high-visibility areas such as inside the door or near the front board or clock?

3. To what extent is there evidence of pushout culture at your school, and how might your classroom décor signal a continuation or disruption of that culture?

4. How might you engage in analysis of your current décor with your students and/or colleagues? Some questions you might ask are:

   a. What messages might my classroom décor be sending to my students—about who they are, who they can become, and who is important?

   b. Is students' work featured?

   c. Are there images of people who look like my students?

   d. If I have motivational posters, what is their tone toward students? What assumptions are they making about students' character or values?

   e. Taken together, is my décor focused more on students' strengths or deficits?

   f. Are there pushout artifacts, and if so, can I remove or visually de-emphasize them?

5. What message is my classroom décor sending about who I am as an equity-oriented teacher? What aspects of an equity orientation (using Figure 1.2, for example) might I want to make more visible, for myself and for others who visit my classroom?

6. Do I already have pivotal artifacts in my classroom to help me remain oriented toward and energized in equity work? Are they serving this purpose effectively? What, if anything, could I add or change so that I can use my classroom décor to help me pivot toward equity more effectively?

CHAPTER 3

Impromptu Teacher/Student Interactions

The Most Important Classroom Texts

> Virtue is not to be discovered in the conduct of the strong vis-à-vis the powerful, but rather it is to be found in our behavior and policies affecting those who are different, those who are weaker, or smaller than we. How do the strong, the powerful, treat children? (Jordan, 2002, p. 270)

The NETS teachers, like many of the best equity-oriented teachers I've observed, carry the heavy burden of ensuring that each of the students entrusted to them will be successful. As discussed in Chapter 1, the NETS teachers shared with me that they experienced a near-constant sense of failing the students who seemed to need them the most although they were devoting extra time, attention, and resources on them. They connected this sense of failing "students who fell through the cracks" to the much-feared, career-ending "burnout" that they know often is experienced by new and justice-oriented teachers. They understood that when teachers are successful in preventing students from falling through the cracks, they feel successful, like they matter; yet when students do fall through the cracks, their teachers are more likely to fall through the cracks too, because they feel like failures.

Heather, Jasmine, Melanie, and Veronica were seriously concerned about the success of about 47% of their students—those we categorized as focal students—and so the sheer volume of work of attending to them is extraordinarily challenging, to say nothing of the other factors clamoring for a teacher's attention. Translating this average percentage to a classroom size of 25 makes it easier to visualize: The teachers were seriously concerned, on average, about the success of 12 students in a 25-student class. When this number is multiplied by the number of classes each teacher teaches, it quickly becomes clear how long her mental "priority" list is—a list overflowing with the innumerable details needed to monitor individual students' progress toward success, including their grades; when they were absent, why, and what they missed; their plans to make up or turn in work; and the teacher's history of communication with their families.

For both teachers and students, the traditional markers of "success" usually include things like grades, test scores, retention rates, and graduation rates—all of which are important to consider. But what is arguably just as important but infinitely more difficult to measure are the human interactions (Greene, 1993), the daily events that, together, lead to these outcomes. This chapter focuses on what transpires within spontaneous human interactions in the classroom and new ways of conceptualizing their "success."

THE SIGNIFICANCE OF IMPROMPTU CLASSROOM INTERACTIONS

Two harmful myths about education often have prevented adequate attention from being paid to teacher/student interactions. The first is a misleading emphasis on "classroom management," in which is embedded a deficit notion of adolescence. Like other programs that prepare students for human service–oriented careers such as in healthcare or law, teacher preparation programs usually do not include a specific focus on how to interact with the humans they will be serving other than in a "classroom management" unit of instruction or course. The notion of classroom management, however, positions students as little more than people who need to be managed, a positioning that relies on negative perceptions of adolescents (Sarigianides, Lewis, & Petrone, 2015). People typically do not enter the teaching profession because they think of teaching in terms of management or because they want to preside over a roomful of individuals all forced to behave the exact same way. Instead, it is much more likely that they enter the teaching profession because they are looking forward to getting to know unique human beings, building relationships with them, and helping them succeed, all through one-on-one interactions.

The second myth is a dehumanizing notion of educational places as corporate spaces. The negative results of corporate language and frameworks invading education have been well documented (Ahlquist, Gorski, & Montaño, 2011; Saltman, 2009); yet this notion continues to position teachers as transmitters of knowledge (Freire, 1970/2000), the work of teaching as "delivery" of "content," and, worst of all, students as "widgets" (Sibilia, cited in Dobo, 2014). Corporate-driven hyper-accountability in education, with its metrics obsession, conceptualizes students and teachers, the human beings at the center of education, as inconvenient, unpredictable variables, impatiently pushing aside notions of care and emphasis on human interactions as quaint reminders of what teaching used to involve.

At the same time, teacher preparation programs rightly spend a great deal of time focusing on lesson and unit planning, and on determining what objectives students should meet and what activities will help them meet those objectives, but teachers also are always engaged in human interactions. In the real world of the classroom, most teacher interactions with individual students are *reactive*; in other words, they are not part of the work that teachers plan for. While certainly equity-oriented teachers plan with students' knowledge, skills, and personalities in mind, most of the one-on-one interactions between teachers and students during class time are improvised. Thus, ironically, most of the interactions that teachers have with their students are never addressed by teacher preparation or professional development programs. Yet these spontaneous interactions between

> Ironically, most of the interactions that teachers have with their students are spontaneous and never addressed by teacher preparation or professional development programs.

teachers and students during class time—interactions that constitute the majority of both teachers' and students' experiences in school—are likely to be highly consequential, particularly for those who are considering leaving school for good. One way that teachers can fight against both pushout culture and myths that dehumanize education is to consciously center their work on the human interactions that serve as the foundation of all teaching and learning.

Positioning Toward Retention as a "Thickening" Text

The ways that, during their interactions, new high school teachers and 9th and 10th graders orient themselves toward staying in or leaving school can be considered through the lens of positioning theory, which focuses on how "people [continually] construct self and other through discursive practices" (McVee, Brock, & Glazier, 2011, p. 4). In the context of school, both teachers and students work to position themselves, while at the same time navigating the ways that they are being positioned by the school context, which often involves positioning them as unwelcome or temporary visitors via pushout culture. Wortham (2004) explains that positioning occurs when "a recognizable category of identity gets explicitly or implicitly applied to an individual in an event that takes place across seconds, minutes, or hours" (p. 166). His research demonstrates how, in a classroom, such positioning can result in a "thickening" of identity, "as the individual and others come increasingly to think of and position him or her as a recognizable kind of person" (p. 166). Building on these notions, this chapter considers that when a teacher and a student are talking to each other in a particular moment, they not only are performing their current selves, but also are laying a foundation for their future selves. The question this chapter considers is: How can teachers interact with their students in ways that position both of them as individuals who will stay in school and succeed there?

Studying the Curriculum of Talk

When I observed English classes for this study, I defined an *interaction* between a student and a teacher as *a discrete, observable, one-on-one social exchange in which significant meaning-making occurs.* I was interested in who initiated each interaction and whether it was based on "a piece of writing" (Brandt & Clinton, 2002, p. 342) or not. My interest in distinguishing between interactions that focused on school curriculum or some form of reading or writing (Gee, 1996) and interactions that did not stems from my desire to observe and analyze how teachers and students move in and out of "school" discourses frequently and fluidly—and how these patterns may differ among groups of students.

As many scholars (e.g., Kirkland, 2013; Lewis, Enciso, & Moje, 2007) note, language, literacy, and sociocultural practices are intertwined. Scholarship on classroom literacy practices and events frequently discusses the relationship between students' official and unofficial literacies (Maybin, 2007) or script and counterscript (Gutierréz, Rymes, & Larson, 1995), as well as between their out-of-school and in-school literacies (Hull & Schultz, 2001). In many cases, these studies position teachers' discourse as script or official, and students' discourse as counterscript or unofficial. This chapter, however, takes a slightly different approach and instead considers the entire body of teacher/student interactions as a social whole, with the understanding that as teachers interact with students over the course of a class period, a semester, or a school year, they weave in and out of official, academics-focused, school-based literacies and unofficial, more personal, counterscript literacies. Teachers' participation in the latter is not something that typically is researched, yet these interactions, like the visual texts described in Chapter 2, form important contexts for learning and for positioning toward retention. Maxine Greene (1993) argues that "persons marked as unworthy are unlikely to feel good enough to pose the questions in which learning begins, unlikely to experience whatever curriculum is presented as relevant to their being in the world" (p. 212). Teachers are uniquely positioned to mark youth as worthy, and they do this important work through their daily interactions with students.

THE ANALYSIS OF CLASSROOM INTERACTIONS

Teachers obviously don't know which of their students are going to pass, fail, or graduate, nor do new teachers know whether they themselves will still be classroom teachers beyond the critical 5-year mark. When I collected the original classroom data for this study, of course, I too didn't know what the future would hold for the teacher participants or their 9th or 10th graders.

The Benefit of Hindsight

Exit interviews with the new teachers, as well as follow-up studies conducted about 8 years after the original study, allowed for the benefit of hindsight in retroactively analyzing their interactions with students. As previously mentioned, all four of the new teachers did go on to remain in the classroom for many years. Further, out of the 125 students in the original study, 100% of the 67 non-focal students passed English for the year, and, of the 58 focal students, 47 (81%) passed and 11 (19%) did not. These percentages suggest that Heather, Jasmine, Melanie, and Veronica were not only accurate in their categorization of focal and non-focal students, but also successful in their work with both focal and non-focal students.

The follow-up study revealed further insights about the 4-year graduation status of the 92 9th-graders in the original study. As Figure 3.1 illustrates, 84 (91%) of the 9th graders passed English (35 focal students and 49 non-focal students), of whom 73 (87%) graduated from high school in 4 years, 11 (13%) transferred out of the district, and 0 (0%) dropped out. Eight 9th graders (19%) did not pass English during the year of the original study. Of these, two (25%) graduated from high school in 4 years, two (25%) transferred to another school district, and four (50%) dropped out. No student in the follow-up study who had dropped out went on to graduate by the 7-year mark. Overall, the results of the follow-up study demonstrate several strong relationships between passing 9th-grade English and graduating from high school, between being identified as a focal student and failing 9th-grade English, and between failing 9th-grade English and dropping out of high school. These findings confirm other research on the importance of 9th grade in school retention (e.g., Allensworth & Easton, 2007; Neild et al., 2001).

The remainder of this chapter demonstrates what happens when these numerical outcomes, together with the teachers' perspectives about them as gathered in exit interviews and follow-up surveys, are used as a lens through which to look closely at teachers' interactions with focal students. That is, the chapter uses what we know about these teachers' and students' eventual futures to retroactively interpret their spontaneous classroom interactions in 9th- and 10th-grade English class. I argue that teachers can use daily improvisational interactions with their students to cultivate a pull-in culture for both themselves and their students—and that a retention curriculum is present in the text of all teacher/student interactions.

Patterns in Teachers' Interactions with Focal Students

Through my study of interactions, I wanted to learn whether there were any differences in how equity-oriented teachers interacted with their focal students and with their non-focal students. Although I initially found that

Figure 3.1. 9th Graders' Passing English and 4-Year Graduation Rates

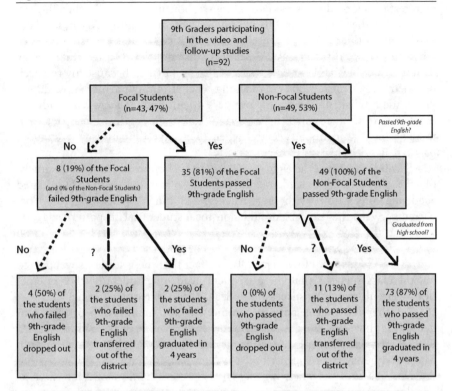

teachers interacted with students in both categories at equal rates, a closer look revealed that there was a high degree of variance in the kind of interactions the teachers had with the focal students, a variance that disappeared when I separated the focal students into two groups using results from one of the follow-up studies: those who passed English for the year and those who didn't. Clear differences in the teachers' interactions with students from the two groups then became apparent.

In the original study, the eight focal students who failed English for the year were spread out across classes and schools. Compared with the larger group of 35 focal students who passed English for the year, the eight were, as a group, absent more frequently, with some of those absences due to suspensions. All eight were students of color, and all were 9th graders in the original study; about half were female, and half were male. The teachers shared with me that almost all of the eight had experienced tragedies and/or had other difficulties in their lives, such as losing a parent or sibling to gun violence and/or serving as caretakers of family members, such as a bedridden parent or their own newborn baby. The teachers confided that they were unsuccessful, despite their best efforts, in establishing a supportive partnership with the parents or guardians of the eight students—likely one of many manifestations of the losses, caretaking responsibilities, and other life circumstances the students and their families were navigating. When teachers reach out to their focal students' families positively and persistently, even when they have difficulty establishing partnerships with the families, they demonstrate powerful commitments to equity. Further, because my research revealed a relationship between lacking teacher/family partnerships, failing 9th-grade English, and dropping out, it is urgent that teachers with commitments to equity recognize the importance of engaging in radical outreach to their focal students, especially when they have difficulty contacting or partnering with the students' families.

During class time, the eight students had even more in common. Namely, their teachers initiated academic interactions with them—and they initiated academic interactions with their teachers—at much higher rates than occurred between the teachers and the non-focal students. This pattern suggests both that the teachers focused intentionally on this concentrated population during class time and that this small group of students was especially actively engaged and focused. However, sadly, the fact that these students went on to fail the class suggests that these frequent academic student/teacher interactions were ultimately unsuccessful, at least in this particular setting.

Another interaction pattern common to this small group of focal students was that they engaged less frequently in personal, social interactions with their teacher, compared with the focal students who passed English. These frequency data suggest that teachers should learn to notice whether they find themselves initiating higher-than-average academic interactions and lower-than-average personal interactions with any of their focal students. If so, the teachers immediately should begin altering their future interactions using strategies suggested in the remainder of this book, so that they can begin positioning both themselves and their students more positively toward retention.

THE HUMANE FOUNDATION OF, AND THE CRACKS IN, TEACHERS' INTERACTIONS WITH FOCAL STUDENTS

In this section, I want to zero in on examples of classroom interactions with the focal students that teachers, particularly new teachers, initially might regard as difficult or challenging because they both represent departures from the lesson they have planned and involve the students whose success they are most concerned about. These interactions often occur, for example, when a student doesn't understand the material, appears not to be working, doesn't have a required material or assignment, does something that the teacher perceives as distracting or disrespectful, asks to leave the room, or becomes frustrated or angry about an assignment or a grade.

My analysis of equity-oriented teachers' classroom interactions with their focal students revealed both the foundation for these interactions and cracks in that foundation. Overall, during challenging interactions with their focal students, equity-oriented teachers work against their school's pushout culture by responding to students humanely, a practice that positions themselves and their students positively toward retention. Equity-oriented teachers respond humanely in several ways, primarily by establishing a foundation of radical patience and radical compassion, which sometimes involves bending school rules. When teachers involved in challenging interactions focus on addressing an individual student's underlying issues, the challenges behind the challenges, so to speak, they maintain and even strengthen this foundation, and they position everyone involved positively toward retention. However, when teachers treat challenging moments as moments for "discipline," cracks form in this foundation and in participants' positioning toward retention. In the following section, I describe and provide examples of both patterns in order to help teachers recognize them in their own practice with focal students and work to seal any interactional cracks so that no student falls through them.

Demonstrating Radical Compassion and Radical Patience

> To let your students in, to let them know too much of your personal life, be too buddy buddy with them? I want to show how, even though we say this is a bad thing, it has worked wonders, because I'm able to be more of guide instead of just their teacher. I've had them come to me saying, "I wish you were my big sister," and are requesting me for next year. So that rigid system of detentions and suspensions and write-ups, although in extreme cases of course I will have to use it, but for the most part I'm identifying that this kid isn't doing this just to disrupt the class, there's something else going on. So instead of punishing the symptom, find out what the problem is underlying the symptom and deal with that. (Jasmine, NETS retreat)

The four teacher participants showed a remarkable consistency in demonstrating radical compassion and radical patience regardless of whether they were interacting with focal students who went on to pass English or with those who went on to fail English for the year. I consider their practices "radical" because they go far beyond everyday politeness in which well-meaning teachers, described in Chapter 1, might engage, and because they are examples of teachers actively looking for and taking opportunities to promote and increase equity through outreach to focal students wherever they can, rather than just being passively polite. They are also radical because they occur, frequently, during tense moments in the classroom that would test most teachers' compassion and patience.

One representative interaction between Heather and Dustin illustrates this humane foundation, as well as Jasmine's advice above to focus on whatever is underlying the symptom and avoid punishing the symptom. One third period on a late May morning, Heather had set up stations by taping small papers all around the room for students to visit as part of a review for an upcoming test. She had just finished giving directions for this activity and was passing out materials when she got to the last row. As she counted out the number of papers she needed for this row, she saw Dustin, one of her focal students, with his head down on his arms atop his desk. Some of the other students had already gotten up from their desks and were spreading out around the room; a few were reading directions out loud or asking one another for pens and pencils, and one was laughingly writing on another person's arm.

> Teachers exercise radical compassion and patience when they go beyond everyday politeness, looking for and taking opportunities to create a pull-in culture by reaching out to focal students during tense moments in the classroom.

As Heather stands in front of Dustin's desk and addresses him, he raises his head to respond.

"You okay today?" Heather asks.

"I'm tired," Dustin replies, yawning and stretching.

Heather smiles. "Amen! What did you have, another marathon movie night?"

He pauses for a moment, then responds slowly and cryptically, "No, I was just out for a long time last night."

She doesn't go there, but raises her eyebrows. "Okay. . . . Did you get *some* sleep?"

"Yeah." He nods.

Heather tilts her head to the side. "You thinking of stopping in tomorrow to go over anything for this test, or do you want to see how the day goes?"

"See how the day goes."

"Okay."

Heather began this interaction without any reference to Dustin's head being down or issuing a direction to sit up. Instead, in this brief interaction, she went out of her way to make several humane moves, specifically:

1. Asking him if he was okay—demonstrating compassion
2. Responding "Amen"—affirming his response and establishing something in common with him
3. Referencing a prior conversation about movies—integrating knowledge of his personal life

4. Asking him about sleep—demonstrating further concern for his health
5. Showing interest in working with him to prepare for a test—establishing her availability and concern for his success

Heather's words create "school" as a supportive space for Dustin and position her as a source of support. Her approach here is emblematic of the majority of the four teachers' interactions with their focal students, resisting a "disciplinary" approach that would invoke rules, expectations, or consequences, and instead demonstrating compassion and patience in ways that strengthen their relationship with one another and their positioning toward retention.

Teachers' demonstration of compassion and patience also can be radical when they are giving focal students the gifts of time and attention amid the swirl of classroom activity, competing and simultaneous demands from multiple students, and the numerous pressures to achieve that they and their students are facing. An interaction between Melanie and Laila on an early February morning illustrates this aspect of equity-oriented teachers' foundation. During a class discussion of the characters Montresor and Fortunato in Poe's "The Cask of Amontillado," Melanie asked a question and received a response she likely would not have anticipated:

"Who is the antagonist, versus the protagonist?" Melanie asks. "Think about it before you answer; have a rationale."

Laila quickly responds, "Maybe he said something about his momma. If you talk about my momma, you going down. Even though I don't like her."

"I'm sorry to hear that," Melanie sympathizes. "That makes me sad."

What makes Melanie's discursive move here radically humane is that she puts her lesson plan on hold for a moment to respond to a student as a human being. It pains me to say this, because such a move shouldn't be radical, but it is: Every moment of class time is precious, carefully planned, and, these days, high-stakes. While it may seem counterintuitive to recommend acknowledging a student's personal comment rather than bringing the conversation back on topic as quickly as possible, this humane approach boldly demonstrates teachers' respect for students. The demonstration of respect makes the approach even more radical when it occurs within a push-out culture that typically makes students feel disrespected. Melanie's move communicated that what the student said was worthy of response, that the teacher was actively listening, even that the student is more important than the lesson.

The foundation of radical compassion and respect on which the teachers based their interactions with focal students, however, does not translate into being a doormat or letting chaos reign in their classroom. Nor does it mean that every time teachers want to address a focal student's actions, they should aim to make a personal connection or demonstrate empathy. In the above two cases, as in the many others I observed, Heather and Melanie did so when a focal student commented on life outside of school. In other cases, when students' actions in the classroom didn't appear to be linked to their lives outside the classroom, equity-oriented teachers redirected students quickly, respectfully, and simply, with a positive tone and sometimes with humor. In my experience, interactions in this category frequently occurred with focal students who went on to pass English for the year and typically followed the teachers' observation that students were talking with others instead of working independently. Focal students who went on to fail English for the year participated in these interactions far less frequently. Looking at such interactions with the understanding that they are always positioning participants with respect to retention suggests that when focal students are talking with others rather than working, they actually are highly engaged socially and therefore positioning themselves positively toward retention.

Through this lens, students' socialization with others, even when they're not working on a teacher-assigned activity, while annoying to the teacher and distracting to others, may be seen as positive and compassionate, perhaps valuing the long term over the short term. At the same time, when equity-oriented teachers respond positively, quickly, simply, and respectfully to students who are talking rather than working, they position themselves positively toward retention as well, since such an approach is consistent with their humane foundation and allows them to focus their time and energy on more substantive matters and to avoid a time- and energy-draining focus on "discipline." A representative compilation of teachers' responses to focal students' talking that are consistent with a humane foundation appears below:

Jasmine: Well, since you have to write a paper eventually, it would be helpful if you wrote something down.
Veronica: Khalil, turn around. Do not prevent Paul from getting his education.
Melanie: Ladies, are you talking or writing?
Veronica: I don't want to write you up.
Heather: I do not want to kill your career as a tattoo artist, but . . .
Veronica: Your next step is for me to move your desk next to mine.
Melanie: Well, that's definitely not appropriate.
Heather: David, that seat's calling your name.
Veronica: You know, this is the reason you have assigned seats.

Another kind of teachers' interaction with focal students provided evidence of radical patience. In these interactions, as in Heather's with Dustin and Melanie's with Laila above, teachers give their focal students the gifts of their undivided time and attention in an environment when many factors are competing for them. What makes interactions in this category radical, in addition to the characteristics mentioned above, is that the focal students often take much more time, or much less time, to complete an assignment than the other students in the class, both of which can place pressure on the teacher's lesson plan. Again, these kinds of interactions were common for both the focal students who went on to pass English for the year and those who didn't.

The example below illustrates a common scenario in which a focal student completes an in-class assignment much too quickly, in the teacher's estimation. It occurred during a mid-March class period with challenging beginnings: Several students had trickled in separately with late passes as Melanie gave directions and passed out an open-book quiz on a novel they were reading, and multiple students were complaining about having to take a quiz.

> The classroom is quiet as all of the students are working on the quiz, and Amiée raises her hand, causing Melanie to approach Amiée's desk.
> "All finished," Amiée states plainly as she hands her quiz to Melanie.
> "Did you answer everything?" Melanie whispers, looking over the paper.
> "No, I didn't do all of them." Amiée shakes her head.
> Melanie calmly hands the quiz back to Amiée. "Well, you're not done."
> "I don't know them," Amiée responds, widening her eyes in protest.
> "You need to try," Melanie urges. "In the directions, it says, 'Try your best!' and it says, 'to get full credit,' so you just wanna try. You don't want to leave anything blank."
> Amiée sighs.
> "You need to try," Melanie repeats.

In Melanie's gradebook, the zeroes next to Amiée's name on the majority of assignments in the marking period to this point reveal, in part, the roots of Melanie's concern for Amiée's success; Amiée had been absent frequently and hadn't made up the assignments she'd missed. This interaction with Amiée demonstrates how teachers patiently and compassionately, but also firmly, can encourage focal students to maximize opportunities to improve their grade during class time, particularly when students have been absent. With their words, teachers can create a sense of hopefulness and of belief in the potential of their students, both of which position teachers and students positively toward retention.

As noted above, sometimes focal students, particularly those with learning differences or those who are English language learners, also take longer to complete in-class assignments than the time teachers have allocated. Such situations can be challenging for teachers when they simultaneously are getting the majority of students started with their next activity and attending to the focal student(s) who are still working. In the example below, Melanie demonstrated radical patience in working with Cliff, a quiet focal student who had near-perfect attendance, mostly failing grades, and no zeroes in Melanie's gradebook. Here, during a class period in which the class was writing an essay, Melanie, while walking around and helping students, noticed that Cliff was sitting quietly, pencil on his desk and hands in his lap.

Melanie sits down at a desk in front of Cliff to address him amid many other students' talking with one another and Antonio loudly trying to convince her to give him extra credit.

"Okay, were you here? Where's your paper?" Melanie asks Cliff.

"I don't know," he responds.

"So that's what you should be doing now. So you can't sit here and not do anything, 'cause that's not gonna help you. So I don't wanna go through your stuff . . ." She opens Cliff's binder and indicates that he should start looking through it, which he does.

Keijah interrupts with, "Miss Davis, you need some more staples!" Melanie gets up to get some, then returns to Cliff, attempting momentarily to ignore Keijah's complaints about the stapler not working and Antonio's requests that she also help him.

Melanie addresses Cliff again. "So what are we doing? Where are your organizers that we did on Tuesday?"

"I don't know," Cliff replies. "Somewhere. I did it, but I don't know where it is."

"Well, you gotta find it. You gotta keep organized. 'Cause if not, it's gonna be hard, 'cause then you have to keep starting over. So if you can't find it, what do you think is the next thing that you should do?"

"Redo it?"

"You don't necessarily have to redo the whole thing if you remember, do you remember the topic that you thought about writing about?"

Cliff shakes his head.

"So then you probably will have to start over. So do you have a folder for this class?"

Cliff taps a folder on his desk.

"Did you look through everything to be sure?"

Cliff looks through the folder as Melanie stands back up and is immediately met with a rush of questions that other students had been waiting to ask her during her time with Cliff.

Although this interaction occurred in March, Melanie persisted in focusing on Cliff's organizational skills, an issue she saw as undermining his success, as Jasmine advises in her earlier comment. When teachers focus on underlying issues like this, they are enacting an equity orientation because they are meeting students at their point of need when it would be easier for them to silently blame students' previous teachers for not addressing the underlying issues, dust them under the pedagogical rug, and proceed as if they weren't a concern. Additionally, when teachers focus on focal students' underlying issues, they are likely helping the students with all of their subjects, not just their own, and thus they are increasing the chances that students will view "school" as a place in which they can be successful. In doing so, teachers also magnify their influence, which in turn can make them feel more efficacious and likely to remain teachers.

A final category illustrating equity-oriented teachers' foundation of radical compassion and radical patience in their interactions with focal students is their willingness to bend school rules when doing so might help their focal students succeed in school. While the bending of rules illustrated below was relatively minor, the fact that the teachers were all pre-tenured raised their level of perceived risk significantly, and yet they engaged in this risk-taking to advocate for their focal students. The two representative interactions described below were told to me by the teachers during their exit interviews:

> *Jasmine:* I had to break school policy to get Dex to stay on task. [She uses a different tone to imitate an administrator:] "There are no electronic devices allowed in class." I would have him pull his phone out, go to his calendar, write the assignment in there, and set an alert. That was the only way I got him on task. It worked. He never missed anything else after that. . . . [But] when I started to go, "The [paper planner] agenda's not working, so you're gonna have to use your phone," he's going, "You're gonna take it!" I said, "I'm not gonna take it!" [chuckles] I really wish they would be flexible with that policy because that worked for quite a few of my students. My seniors too! We would be like, "Pull out your devices! Let's synch!"
>
> *Heather:* But yeah, Paul showed up 20 minutes late for the final. I was counting [students]. I said, "Where is Paul?" And Taylor asked, "Can I call him?" I was like, "No, but you can go and use the bathroom." So he did, and he called him; Taylor came back in, and he was like, "He's leaving now." Then he showed up.

Perhaps no interaction with focal students could communicate more powerfully that their teacher cares about their success and that their success is possible than teachers bending school rules for them. While Jasmine could have chosen to let Dex continue to miss deadlines without intervening or to chide him to get his act together, and while Heather could have chosen to let Paul miss the final without intervening, these teachers chose to intervene. These teachers' moves provide powerful examples of interactions made in opposition to pushout culture; in fact, interactions like this actively create a pull-in culture, one in which teachers eschew "discipline" like zero-tolerance policies in favor of doing what they can to help students succeed.

Identifying Cracks in the Foundation

Tasked with identifying the reasons why focal students still fell through the cracks despite the teachers' best efforts, however, I sought to identify patterns when the teachers' foundation of radical compassion and radical patience cracked in their interactions with focal students. As noted briefly above, I found that cracks appeared whenever teachers treated challenging moments with their focal students as moments for "discipline." Most important, I found that, across all four teachers and all 125 students, across all seven classes in all four schools, these interactions involved only the eight students who went on to fail English for the year. In other words, analysis revealed that the teachers at times interacted differently with the students who went on to pass and with the students who went on to fail English for the year. While these kinds of interactions were rare, and while the teachers could not know at the time their students' eventual outcomes, the correlation between these interactions and those outcomes suggests that avoiding such interaction patterns with their focal students may be an effective way of positioning the students and themselves for successful retention in school.

An illustration of the difference in interactions between "firm foundation" and "cracks in the foundation" appears in Table 3.1. This table names two classroom situations—a student covertly texting and a student throwing balled-up paper toward but missing the trash can—that were relatively common among focal students during my observations. Alongside each situation appear examples of teachers' contrasting responses representing the larger pattern I observed. In the first situation, when focal students who went on to pass English were covertly texting, teachers would say things like, "Painfully obvious," maintaining a foundation of compassion and patience, and even using humor. But when focal students who went on to fail English were covertly texting, teachers would make moves toward discipline. In the same way, when focal students who went on to pass English missed the trash can, teachers would respond supportively or even with encouragement, while with focal students who went on to fail English, they would respond with rules, commands, or reprimands.

A similar table could be constructed using the examples that appear earlier in this chapter, with one row contrasting Heather's responses of "You okay today?" and "Did you get *some* sleep?" to Dustin with his head down on his desk, with responses like, "Get up," "Let's get moving," or "Wake up, Dustin." Another row could contrast Melanie's response of "I'm sorry to hear that. That makes me sad" to Laila's comment about her mother with responses like, "Stay on topic," or "That's enough, Laila."

Interactions like those in the righthand column of Table 3.1 bear all the hallmarks of pushout culture, which, as previously discussed, is characterized by a negative environment, harsh discipline and criminalization of students, unsupportive teachers and staff, feelings of fear and hopelessness,

Table 3.1. Interactional Differences in the Smallest Places

Classroom Situation	Foundation: Teacher's Response to a Focal Student Who Passed	Crack in the Foundation: Teacher's Response to a Focal Student Who Failed
Student is covertly texting.	"Painfully obvious."	"Give me your phone."
Student throws balled-up paper toward trash can and misses.	"That was close."	"Come pick that up; you know I don't let you throw anything into the trash from your seat."

and being negatively perceived and/or perceiving others negatively. No equity-oriented teacher, including Heather, Jasmine, Melanie, and Veronica, would intentionally be unsupportive or promote pushout culture. Rather, they would aim for the opposite—a fact that suggests that if they, or any other equity-oriented teacher, engage in interactions like this, they do so unwittingly. It therefore becomes of utmost importance for teachers and those who support them to learn how to identify these interactions and the contexts in which they typically occur, so that they can be prevented and replaced with the kinds of interactions that are consistent with the compassionate, patient foundations of equity-oriented interactions with focal students. Doing this work can help fill the cracks through which focal students—and their often-new teachers—frequently fall.

One important commonality across these challenging moments is that they represent rare moments when an equity-oriented teacher was running on empty—compassion drained, patience thin. The reason for *this* kind of teacher shortage (the kind that often silently precedes the teacher shortages that appear in headlines) was often a combination of pressure—due to the heightened importance of class time for focal students, who were frequently absent—and repetition—due to repeatedly addressing students when they didn't respond as desired to the teachers' direction(s) earlier in the class period, as well as over the course of their time together in class. In this way, the identities of both the focal students and the teachers involved in these interactions became "thickened" as they settled into a negative pushout pattern with one another. Such a phenomenon is hardly newsworthy to adults who have grown weary of repeating themselves when youth in their care don't listen to their initial requests.

Almost all of the negative interactions I observed occurred when the focal students were either doing nothing or doing something other than the in-class work that the teachers had assigned everyone to complete individually at their desks, and these are the interactions on which I focus in this section. The other primary, but less frequent, in-the-cracks pattern I observed, but do not focus on in this section, consisted of the teachers and students not interacting at all. A few of the focal students who went on to fail English for the year, all of whom were female and quieter than their peers, engaged in very few interactions with the teacher: They rarely participated verbally in class discussion or initiated interactions with the teacher, flying almost completely under her radar.

The following chronological series of interactions, one each month over the course of 4 months, shows how one of the teachers and Tyrese, a focal student who went on to fail English for the year, created and re-created a pushout microculture in their interactions. The first example below, which occurred in the first few minutes of class, illuminates Tyrese's zero for this day's journal entry grade in the gradebook. While it began with some parallels to the earlier interaction between Melanie and Amiée, notably the teacher's words, "you're not done," this interaction took a different turn.

> The teacher is circulating among the students, checking their progress. She addresses the class. "Two more minutes of writing! Shhh." As she walks by Tyrese, she notices that he is not writing. "Tyrese, are you finished with your journal? If I came and checked it, it would be fine?"
>
> "Yeah," Tyrese responds with a smile.
>
> "Okay, you got five to eight sentences?"
>
> "No," Tyrese admits.
>
> "Okay, so then you're not done," the teacher prods.
>
> Tyrese begins, "I didn't know . . . ," but the teacher interrupts.
>
> "Which is why you always complain to me about your journals. Five to eight sentences is standard. You guys know that."
>
> "I got one," Tyrese shares enthusiastically. "You said write something; I don't feel like writing that story." He points to the prompt on the screen.
>
> The teacher asks rhetorically, "So what was your other option?" She reminds students often that if they don't want to write on the prompt, they can write whatever is on their mind.
>
> Tyrese clearly remembers this, as he responds with, "There's nothing on my mind."
>
> "Nothing?" the teacher asks. "So you gotta make something up, 'cause when I grade them, it's not gonna be good."

The contrast between this interaction and the earlier "you're not done" interaction between Melanie and Amiée centers on how the students responded to this teacher's push to keep working. Because Amiée accepted Melanie's challenge, their interaction about her test concluded with a positive, supportive, hopeful spirit, providing a satisfying experience of encouragement and thus a positioning toward retention for both Amiée and Melanie. While this teacher's interaction with Tyrese began similarly, it quickly became an interaction not of encouragement but of a student naming multiple reasons why he was not writing (he didn't know that it had to be longer than one sentence; he doesn't want to write about the given prompt, and can't think of anything else to write) and of the teacher responding to each of these reasons in turn (with a length rule, an alternative, and a potential consequence). Thus, while this interaction began with the kind of compassionate outreach that is consistent with the humane foundation of equity-oriented teachers' work with focal students, and while even at the end the teacher was still encouraging the student to work ("you gotta make something up"), its conclusion of "when I grade them, it's not gonna be good" enters pushout territory with its negative outlook and emphasis on consequences.

Another example replicates the positive introduction and negative conclusion of the previous example. During an open-book test about a month later, the teacher saw as she was walking around the room that Tyrese wasn't working. When she approached him, she made the following whispered comments, with brief, inaudible responses from Tyrese interspersed among them:

"You need to open your book and try to answer some of these questions. What did I say before: If you don't know it, you need to skip it, go to the next one, and go back. I watched you sit here. So you need to open the book. How are you going to get the answers if you don't open the book? So what, so you're just gonna sit here and not do anything?"

Another month later, toward the end of a class held in a computer lab where students were working on a paper, the teacher, who had been circulating among the students, was beginning the transition back to the classroom but, surprised by what she saw on Tyrese's screen, paused to address him accusingly.

The teacher addresses the class: "All right, so whatever it is that you're working on right now, make sure you finish that. If you're typing on the computer—" She stops mid-sentence as she sees that Tyrese is looking up his school attendance records.
   She turns to address him. "What are you doing?" She then lowers her voice. "You are not working on your paper, so close out of that."

Three months after the first journal-related interaction above, the teacher and Tyrese again clash concerning journals at the beginning of class.

Tyrese walks directly from the hallway to the teacher's desk at the beginning of class and picks up a bottle of lotion. "Can I borrow this?" he asks.
   "Sure." She smiles.
   "My legs are really dry," he offers, taking the lotion to his desk and sitting down.

The teacher looks around at the class, addressing them: "All right, take a seat, guys, good morning! Take 5 minutes to work on your journal."

Four minutes into the journal, she addresses Tyrese. "It does not take you 4 minutes to put lotion on your legs. And you missed your journal."

"I was really ashy," Tyrese replies, causing some students to laugh.

The teacher chuckles during her first word, then quickly turns serious: "And you missed your journal. It should not take you 4 minutes to put lotion on."

The examples above offer important glimpses into how the humane foundation of equity-oriented teachers' radical compassion and patience can, like any other foundation, experience stressors that eventually cause cracks. These examples show how a gradual erosion of compassion and patience can cause even equity-oriented teachers to unwittingly create a *pushout microculture*, which I define as a space within a school setting—as small as a student's relationship with a teacher—characterized by thickened negative language, dispositions, and positioning away from retention. This notion of pushout microculture draws from scholarship on educational microcultures (e.g., Banks, 2004; Gilbert & Yerrick, 2001) as well as on pushout (e.g., Tuck, 2011) in order to locate identifiable "components inside schools that detain and derail students' secondary school completion" (p. 818).

The dialogues in the latter part of this chapter provide real-life examples of what can constitute pushout culture writ large: dozens of pushout microcultures in students' relationships with school staff, including teachers, over days, weeks, months, years, classrooms, schools—pushout microcultures that can be created inadvertently even by equity-oriented teachers. If we consider that this relationship is but one of many Tyrese has had in schools by this point in his life, and if we hypothesize that his other interactions in these relationships might have been similar, it is easy to see how leaving school could begin to feel inevitable. At the same time, when any teachers, particularly teachers committed to working for social justice, find themselves becoming negative, discipline-oriented, and unsupportive in their interactions with students, they are likely to question their efficacy—rightly so—and therefore their "fit" in the field.

CONCLUSION: FILLING THE CRACKS IN THE FOUNDATION

This chapter argues that during class time, teachers can use their interactions with the students about whose success they're concerned to catch them before they fall through the cracks. Understanding how to engage in this important work during the precious, chaotic minutes of a class period is critical for equity-oriented teachers' efficacy, as those minutes represent the time during which teachers have the most opportunities and the most agency.

What would it take to fill the cracks in the foundation of equity-oriented teachers' interactions with their focal students? One answer, of course, is policy, although this book intentionally is addressed to teachers wishing to take equity matters into their own hands without waiting for policy change to occur. So while, of course, policy changes, such as reduced class sizes and increased funds for staff to assist with family outreach and language translation, would help increase teachers' efficacy, the patterns identified in this chapter can provide guidance for new and equity-oriented teachers. Below, I offer teachers recommendations for overcoming obstacles and engaging in a critical analysis of their own during-class interactions in order to create a pull-in culture with their own focal students.

Obstacle #1: Disrupting Pushout Microculture in Progress

While pushout microcultures do take time to develop, once that pattern of development has begun, teachers may wonder how to curb it and, further, to transform their interactions to pull-in microcultures. If the train has left the station, how can we alter its course? I suggest the following for teachers engaged in interaction patterns that have become negative:

- Examine your upcoming curriculum for openings through which you can invite and engage students' personal lives. Personal connections are an important antidote for pushout microcultures, and teachers who construct curriculum that centers on student knowledge and experiences not only create such connections but lay the foundation for future positive, compassionate, patient individual interactions. Jasmine, for example, assigns a personal narrative at the beginning of the school year to establish this connection, and such assignments can be integrated throughout the year.
- Examine your classroom routines to locate or create ways to engage in regular, one-on-one interactions with each of your students during class time. One common strategy I observed among the NETS teachers is to assign students to work on an activity individually or in groups, and to circulate, making notes on each student's progress during this time. Otherwise, too many days can pass without interacting one-on-one with a student— which is particularly important for focal students.

Obstacle #2: Responding to the "Tough Love" Myth

Well-meaning teachers and others working with youth, particularly urban youth of color, at times reject compassion and patience as soft and instead favor a rules-toting, tough love approach, with the reasoning that it is consistent with the tough contexts youth navigate. But studies (e.g., Flett, Gould, Griffes, & Lauer, 2013) find tough love approaches ineffective, and critiques of punitive approaches to teaching youth in poverty argue that "children raised in poverty display ample amounts of grit every day, and they don't need more of it in school" (Ris, 2016; see also Duncan, 2000). Rather, the kinds of interactions with teachers that youth most need in these times of racial violence are those soaked in compassion and patience, consistent with "classrooms as sites for healing and racial justice" (Baker-Bell, Butler, & Johnson, 2017, p. 125). For teachers tempted to interact with their focal students using "tough love" instead of compassion and patience, I recommend the following:

- Start small, then grow quickly. Although making changes to the ways that you approach your focal students may be difficult at first, as you may struggle with anger or impatience, try focusing on your interactions with just one of your focal students. This approach will help you gain skill and confidence before you make broader changes, which you should then be able to make much more quickly.
- Take a moment. In challenging situations such as those described in this chapter, the words that first occur to you to use in your response may not be positive or encouraging. I urge teachers resolved to create a pull-in culture in their interactions with focal students to develop the skill of critically examining what they plan to say before they say it, taking a few seconds to reflect before responding in the heat of the moment.

QUESTIONS FOR TEACHER REFLECTION, DISCUSSION, AND ACTION

1. Who are your focal students? You can't improve your work with your focal students without knowing exactly who they are. Make a list of your focal students. Feel free to use, revise, or improve the criteria that we used in NETS: Focal students (a) have a D or an F average in English; (b) engage in activities that research cites as indicative of high "at risk" for dropout—such as being absent frequently, not turning in work, not participating in class, and being disruptive; and/or (c) are students that you feel you are not reaching despite your best efforts.

2. What history do you have with each of your focal students? Take some time to construct and reflect on the interactional history you are creating with each of your focal students. Include the last few things each of you has said to the other, the kinds of interactions you typically have, or topics you typically discuss, as close to word for word as you can.

3. Make a list of what you know personally about each of your focal students: What makes them unique? What are their talents, interests, areas of brilliance? If you are not sure, determine a specific day and time when you can reach out to your focal student(s) to talk individually with them or to attend a school event in which they are participating and connect with them there.

4. How might you engage in analysis of your interactions with your students and/or colleagues? You might ask yourself the following: To what extent do my interactions tend toward valuing others as human beings? Being focused on discipline? Being characterized by compassion, patience, or encouragement? Being characterized by negativity or discouragement?

5. Based on the above analyses, how can you improve your current interactions with your focal students so that they more powerfully reflect your equity orientation? To accomplish these improvements, make a list of specific changes you can make in the content and delivery of your words toward your focal students, and specific days and times that you will commit to making these changes.

6. Who can support you in making changes? Consider partnering with other teachers who also teach your focal students in order to collaboratively determine effective interactions and to hold one another accountable in using more radically patient, compassionate approaches.

CHAPTER 4

The Crucial Curriculum of Before and After Class

It remains a matter, for men and women both, to establish a place for freedom in the world of the given—and to do so in concern and with care, so that what is indecent can be transformed and what is unendurable may be overcome. (Greene, 1988, p. 86)

In this chapter, I propose that the moments leading up to and immediately following class time offer unique and critically important opportunities for equity-oriented teachers to interact with their students. With reference to Maxine Greene's words above, before- and after-class moments represent a critical "place for freedom in the world of the given"—a place apart from "the given" of "English class," where standards, curriculum, assessments, lesson plans, and even seating charts govern teachers' work. Whether the first three of these are "indecent" or "unendurable" is certainly a heated debate; however, there is no doubt that they are increasingly "given" to teachers, significantly decreasing teachers' agency and opportunities to exercise their professional discernment. In Chapter 3, I described how teachers can enact a commitment to social justice and create positionings toward retention in their interactions with students during class time. In this chapter and the next, I focus on the minutes before and after class, when teachers can "establish a place for freedom" for both themselves and their students in ways that, I argue, are not possible during class time. As in previous chapters, I proceed with the understanding that in their interactions, both teachers and students use language to perform and create their identities as well as position themselves and one another with respect to the prospect of remaining in school.

RECOGNIZING THE HYBRID UNIQUENESS OF BEFORE- AND AFTER-CLASS TIMESPACES

The bell signaling the end of class is about to ring. Jasmine starts walking from the front board to her desk in the back, wrapping up class while her students are packing their backpacks and moving toward the door, where they stand until the bell rings.

She stops midway back. "Quick, before you run off, who learned something about love today?"

"Me!" "I did!" many students sing out. Jasmine again starts walking toward her desk when she spots Robyn looking at her phone with two other girls. She leans over Robyn's shoulder and looks at the phone, too.

"Ooooooh! Hand it over." Jasmine holds out an open hand toward Robyn's phone. The girls all laugh. "She knows I'm playing."

One of the girls, Eleesha, erupts: "Ms. Brown, I told you I was gonna tell you a secret!"

"What's the secret?" Jasmine asks.

"Come!" Eleesha motions for Jasmine to follow her to the back of the room, and she does. Eleesha faces the back wall, away from everyone, and talks quietly but excitedly. "I wrote this poem, and it was, like, really nice. And I read it to my whole family, and it's like, it's really emotional, and I want you to read it. So you can hang it up on your wall."

"Really!?" Jasmine gushes.

"But I don't want the whole class to know," Eleesha worries.

"Cool!" Jasmine encourages. "Well, don't put your name on it. Nobody has to know."

"It's really nice," continues Eleesha.

"Just don't put your name on it. I can put it on my poetry wall," Jasmine notes, motioning with her right palm toward the wall.

"It's like the best thing I ever, well, I been writing poetry, like, a lot, and you got me started."

"I did?!?!"

"Yeah."

"Oh, cool!"

"I wrote, like, six poems, and they all rhyme and everything."

"Nice. You know you don't have to rhyme."

"Yeah, I know. I want to be a rapper." Eleesha starts walking up to her desk and picks up her backpack.

"You have it in you. You can." Eleesha joins everyone else standing by the door. The bell rings. Jasmine is now standing mid-room, among the student desks.

She now loudly addresses everyone over the ringing bell. "You know, we have a talent show coming up." Eleesha hangs at the back of the others who are leaving the room. "Eleesha?" Jasmine lightly touches the back of Eleesha's shoulder. "We have a talent show coming up in April. Think you'll be ready?"

"I'm always ready!" Robyn and Thalma remain near Eleesha and slowly walk out with her. Jasmine laughs.

Robyn backs up. "When's that? April?"

Jasmine nods. "Talent show's in April."

"I know what I'm doing," Robyn promises.

"I already know what you gon' do," Jasmine gestures toward Robyn.

"You never know! I might surprise y'all, Ms. Brown! You know me! Always full of surprises!"

Jasmine laughs. "Of course!" The three girls exit the room.

As ungoverned, hybrid spaces within the school day, the moments before and after class provide places for teachers and students to assert their agency and to create or perform their identities in ways that are not possible during class time. In the above interaction, Eleesha, an African American female, takes the opportunity to engage privately with her teacher Jasmine—an opportunity that Jasmine created when she concluded the formal part of her class 2 minutes before the bell rang and made herself available to interact informally with students during unstructured time. In this brief interaction, Jasmine and Eleesha transcend their student and teacher roles by establishing their shared interest in poetry: Jasmine plays the roles of a poet and mentor of poets when she encourages Eleesha and gives her advice about rhyming, and Eleesha performs her identity as a confident, practiced poet. In this powerfully affirming interaction, Eleesha also positions her teacher as someone worthy of a secret and as her inspiration to write poetry. Jasmine's equity orientation is observable in this interaction as she supports and encourages Eleesha in the development of her voice, a key component of social justice– and equity-oriented curriculum. Jasmine and Eleesha connect here as two African American women poets who, as they inspire each other, are creating school as a positive space for themselves as Black females. Because, as Morris (2016) contends, the actions of Black girls increasingly are criminalized in schools, the creation of positive spaces in which students like Eleesha can feel brilliant and valued is a form of equity pedagogy that is urgently needed.

> As ungoverned, hybrid spaces within the school day, the moments before and after class provide places for teachers and students to assert their agency and to create or perform their identities in ways that are not possible during class time.

Jasmine and Eleesha's poetry discussion illustrates how equity-oriented interactions can be facilitated outside of class time by teacher-created classroom décor. As described in Chapter 2, Jasmine's poetry wall communicated both to Jasmine and to her students that writing honestly about one's personal life is valuable and welcomed in this classroom space. Jasmine and Eleesha's conversation illustrates how the unique *time* of "before class" and "after class" can intersect with a teacher's unique, intentionally designed *space* to create the kind of freedom described in Maxine Greene's quotation at the beginning of this chapter.

The scholarship of third space provides an important lens through which to view this intersection, as third space typically is defined as a hybrid space in which the official and unofficial, the formal and informal, school and home, come together (Bhabha, 1994; Moje et al., 2004; Soja, 1996). Before- and after-class time, and the interactions that occur during them, are notable for this hybridity. By definition, they are times of in-between-ness; they occur between class times and between class spaces. They are distinguished by physical movement, as both students and teachers typically occupy different physical spaces than they do during class time. Many teacher/student interactions during these moments occur in hybrid physical spaces: in hallways, inside the classroom doorframe, in the front of the classroom, or along the sides of the classroom.

The notion that space and time are not merely interrelated but inseparable offers an important perspective on before- and after-class teacher/student interactions. Massey (1994) argues that time and space should not be thought of as separate concepts but rather as one singular entity, as "space-time" (p. 269). This idea, also referred to as "timespace" (Compton-Lilly & Halverson, 2014), helps us understand how, when teachers and students engage socially with one another, they are creating a social space, just as the social space they are creating affords different kinds of social practices (Leander & Sheehy, 2004).

Looking at Jasmine and Eleesha's after-class poetry conversation from this perspective reveals how before- and after-class timespaces can function in ways that influence positioning toward retention. When Eleesha leads Jasmine away from the rest of the class, her proximity to the poetry wall allows Jasmine to easily gesture toward it when she says, "I can put it on my poetry wall." Eleesha's choice to locate this private after-class interaction next to the poetry wall positions them both figuratively and literally in relation to it. When Eleesha initiates this interaction with Jasmine about her at-home literacy practices, she both reveals and creates her positive positioning toward retention in this timespace. Jasmine facilitates this orientation by creating the timespace through her poetry wall and a few informal after-class moments. In this brief interaction with Eleesha, Jasmine's practices as an equity-oriented teacher are evident in the margins of traditional classroom practice; this example demonstrates the important possibilities of such timespaces in equity-oriented teaching.

MAKING HUMANE CONNECTIONS
BETWEEN CLASSES AS EQUITY PEDAGOGY

Many of the moves through which teachers commonly enact commitments to social justice involve seeking out, listening to, and responding to students' perspectives and experiences. As Paris and Winn (2014) describe, taking a humanizing approach means prioritizing "relationships of care, dignity, and

~~respect~~" (p. xvi). These moves are both simply and profoundly humanizing in nature, positioning human relationships at the center of the educational experience, making individuals feel acknowledged and valued. A large body of scholarship has agreed that experiencing a sense of belonging in school strongly correlates with retention, both for marginalized students (e.g., Fine, 1991; Finn, 1989; Osterman, 2000; Swaminathan, 2004) and for new teachers, particularly teachers of color and teachers in under-resourced schools (Achinstein et al., 2010; Cochran-Smith, 2004b; Freedman & Appleman, 2009; Ingersoll, 2003). These studies suggest that in order to choose to stay in school, both students and teachers need to feel that they are valued, respected, and supported members of the school community. The before-class timespace offers a particularly promising space for these moves, as does, to a lesser extent, the after-class timespace. While in theory both timespaces would be similarly promising, in reality the after-class timespace typically finds both students and teachers eyeing the clock, readying themselves physically and mentally for whatever is next on their schedule. In contrast, during the before-class timespace, teachers and students often seem more prone to linger, and teachers can take advantage of this natural tendency. I witnessed Melanie, Veronica, Jasmine, and Heather consistently engage in three types of between-class moves that teachers can use to create and strengthen students' connections with them and also with the school setting:

1. Ask questions that demonstrate interest in students' personal lives, and share information about their own personal lives
2. Demonstrate empathy and/or humor when responding to student revelations
3. Use language that positions students and teachers as members of a shared classroom or school community

As will become clear in the sections below, these moves often overlap or occur simultaneously in equity-oriented teachers' talk.

Ask Personal Questions; Share Personal Information

The first aspect of this move is one that many teachers practice between classes as a matter of course. Teachers' most frequent questions or comments in this area often involve students' immediate experiences and range from "How was your weekend?" and "How was your holiday?" to "Did you dye your hair?" "I like your Chucks!" and "What in the world is in your bag?" Because these direct questions typically draw upon shared experiences (weekends, holidays) or students' physical appearance or belongings, they are easy points of entrée for teachers in making connections with students and in helping students feel noticed and valued. Teachers who desire to begin making connections with their students can do so easily by making moves of this type. More advanced variations on this first move become possible when teachers and students have been engaging in sustained interpersonal interactions over time. These moves are evident in teacher questions that reference earlier conversations and show the teacher's interest in the individual student's well-being. For example, following a holiday break, when Jasmine simply asked Terrence, "Still no glasses?" before class, it was clear that they previously had discussed Terrence's need for glasses and that Jasmine was both expressing concern at his not yet wearing them and not-so-subtly urging him to get them and/or begin wearing them. Such a question signals to Terrence that a teacher is noticing him, and can help create a positive positioning toward retention: If school is a place where you feel cared for, you may feel more inclined to return there on a daily basis. At the same time, such a question allows an equity-oriented teacher like Jasmine to feel that she is making a difference in a student's life, simultaneously increasing her own positioning toward retention.

Less frequently, equity-oriented teachers also share personal details about their lives between classes, although this sharing appears to be done not for the purpose of calling attention to themselves but rather to invite students to follow their lead and share as well. Additionally, when teachers express parts of their own personal identities, skills, or interests, they are not only crafting school into a space that is imbued with individual personalities but also further demonstrating to their students that it is a space in which integration of individuals' personalities is welcome. As discussed in Chapter 2, teachers' display of personal artifacts in the classroom can function as another method through which teachers initiate personal interaction with students, much like Jasmine's poetry wall did in her conversation with Eleesha. In the example below, Veronica's move to share a detail of her personal life with Keesha, a female African American student, demonstrates how quickly and naturally students typically respond in kind, even in the midst of a chaotic before-class hallway.

Veronica is standing in the hallway outside her classroom door as students pass her to enter the room before class starts.

Em, entering the room, asks, "You want us to sit in our groups?"

"Yes, ma'am," Veronica answers.

Her attention turns toward Tom, now approaching the door. "Hey, Tom, you sit with your group today, not with me, okay?" He nods and wordlessly enters the room.

Next, she sees Keesha and notices her nails. "Howdy! I'm gonna paint my nails yellow this weekend."

Keesha shakes her head. "I messed mine up. The lady was like, you need to let them dry a little longer, but I didn't feel like it, so they all—"

"So they have like little dents and stuff in them?" Mateo passes them and enters the room.

"Mm hmm," Keesha responds.

Jametta approaches them. "Sit in our groups?" she asks.

"Yeah, sit in your group." Then, to Keesha, she suggests, "Go over it, maybe if you go over it with clear nail polish, you can kind of move it?"

"Mm hmm."

"But they're cute." Mateo, backpack still on, returns to the hallway.

Keesha starts to ask Veronica, "Are you still gonna show me your—" but is interrupted.

"Can I go to the bathroom?" Mateo asks.

Veronica sees Tommy coming down the hall, still pretty far away, and immediately starts laughing. "Hey! What??" Then, turning to Mateo, "Yeah, go."

She turns back toward Tommy. "You have a mohawk? Really? Okay. All right." She blinks several times. Tommy smiles and enters the room. Yolanda now comes toward the door, and Veronica greets her, "Hi, darling."

Diego sneaks up behind Veronica, then jumps in front of her. "Heyyyy! You didn't see me, did you, Miss J? You didn't see me, did you?"

"I didn't!" She raises an eyebrow as an elated Diego returns to the room.

Given the bustle of students in the hall and the number of students exiting and entering the classroom during these times of transition, it initially seemed to me to be a small miracle each time I witnessed teachers making a substantive connection with a student between classes in the middle of it all. Yet it quickly became apparent to me that for these equity-oriented teachers, connecting with students during this timespace was the rule rather than the exception. The fact that the entire example above, for instance, lasted 60 seconds illustrates that teachers need to be quick and improvisational to take advantage of possible openings to connect with students. Here, Veronica invites Keesha to engage in such a connection by sharing a simple detail of her life—that she planned to paint her nails yellow this weekend. Keesha's response, as she shares a brief personal narrative about how her nails got messed up, indicates her trust of and comfort with Veronica. In her offer of advice, Veronica validates Keesha's narrative—and thus, implicitly, Keesha herself—as, through this advice, she both demonstrates that she was listening and establishes the narrative as worthy of serious response. Veronica and Keesha—like many other teachers and students I observed—were able to bond with each other between and even during Veronica's interactions with a number of other students. Although the intrusion of Tommy's hair and Diego's sneak attack prevented them from successfully transitioning into a second topic, the fact that Keesha attempted to continue the conversation indicates her investment in it, another small but telling artifact of a sense of belonging and positive positioning toward retention. The ease with which Veronica also engages in light-hearted talk with Tommy and Diego suggests that the same is true of their individual relationships. The keen level of observation, direction- and advice-giving, joking, and laughing that Veronica demonstrates in this brief timespace points to a professional who not only is confident and capable but also is creating and revealing a sense of enjoyment in her job and a positive positioning toward retention.

Demonstrate Empathy with Humor

The second between-classes move I observed involves teachers responding with empathy and humor when students express frustration, stress, or exhaustion, a fairly common occurrence in the classrooms of the equity-oriented teachers I studied. This kind of move illustrates how teachers' careful listening and thoughtful responding can position students as valued, capable members of a relationship and of a community. Often, such interchanges are extremely brief, like those below, which occurred in succession as students entered Jasmine's room before class. They illustrate how equity-oriented teachers might respond to students who voice, however briefly or trivially, a negative disposition toward retention.

> Jasmine has just finished writing instructions on the front board when Thalma enters the classroom wearing a very bright coral hoodie-and-sweatpants outfit.
>
> She addresses Jasmine, singing, "Hiiiii!"
>
> Jasmine responds approvingly, "Ooooooh! Bright! Hel-LO! You going to spice up Friday?" She follows Thalma toward the back of the room, where Thalma places her bag on her chair, and Jasmine picks up her water bottle from her desk and takes a drink.
>
> Thalma laughs. "Yeah, well, I didn't want to come today."
>
> "Well, I'm glad you did. I'd have been very upset if you didn't come today," Jasmine replies.
>
> "Really?"
>
> "Yes." Many more students enter the room, led by Gwen. Jasmine puts her bottle down, applies hand lotion from her drawer, and starts rubbing her hands together.
>
> Gwen walks purposefully toward Jasmine's desk. "I forgot my permission slip again!"
>
> Jasmine shakes her head. After a moment, she adds, "It's 'cause you don't love me."
>
> "No, I do! I do!" They both laugh.

While such expressions of love for and from students are regular occurrences in Jasmine's teaching practice, the timing and substance of these two examples are particularly illustrative for equity-oriented educators. In both instances, the students offered revelations ("I didn't want to come today" and "I forgot my permission slip again") that were somewhat negative in substance, but in each case Jasmine responded not by asking further questions or reprimanding the students but instead by referring to their close teacher/student relationship ("I'd have been very upset if you didn't come today" and "It's 'cause you don't love me"). With these comments, Jasmine characterizes herself as a teacher for whom student attendance and even submitting forms are personal acts of love. At the same time, Thalma and Gwen, respectively, respond positively to Jasmine's humor. The laughter they share in a brief one-on-one moment with their teacher, because it is one of many such interactions over the course of the year, further cements their relationship and helps create a positive positioning toward retention for both teacher and student. Jasmine's responses to Thalma and Gwen demonstrate that when teachers respond to students' negative dispositions in positive ways rather than with more negativity, they are making powerful moves that can alter both the short-term student/teacher relationship and the long-term relationship with the idea of staying in school.

The example below represents another common pattern of before-class teacher/student interactions, in which a student makes a more significant personal revelation and the teacher responds to it with empathy and/or humor. Here, Heather shows one simple way that teachers who are committed to social justice can create the kind of discursive openings in which students like Crystal, a White female, can share important personal information that is affecting both their school and home life.

> The bell rings, and Heather sits down atop a student desk to face the students. "Have a nice weekend?" she asks. There is a chorus of responses as students joke for a while about going to the beach.
>
> Then Crystal inserts quietly, hesitatingly, "My basement flooded."
>
> Heather gasps. "Really? I'm sorry! Did you lose stuff, or is everything . . . okay?"
>
> "My room's in the basement," Crystal frowns.
>
> "Ohhhh. Crystal, I'm sorry." Heather places her hand over her mouth as she stands up. She adds, "Did you lose, is your, was your book down there? Do you need a new one?"
>
> "No, my book wasn't down there." Hints of a smile emerge on Crystal's face.
>
> "Oh, thank God!" Heather laughs while making an exaggerated "Darn!" gesture, swinging her bent right arm and snapping her fingers on her right hand. Crystal's smile widens. After a brief pause, Heather adds, more seriously now, "Well, let me know how things go, if we need to shift some dates around for you. Um, all right. Here's, here's what's going on today."

Crystal's quiet revelation here demonstrates the human tendency to try to locate even the smallest opening in a social setting to share something important that has happened, like the fact that someone pulled an all-nighter last night, that homecoming planning is driving someone else crazy, or that a loved one just received bad medical news. What these instances have in common is that they seem to come from a desire to be known more holistically, to be understood in a larger context, to connect with another human being about human experiences that go beyond the more fixed identities of "student" and "teacher." In school settings, we as teachers and students share personal information perhaps because we want to explain ourselves, and this explanation functions implicitly to request that others use this information to interpret our dispositions or behavior. Perhaps Crystal wanted Heather to know why she was exhausted or upset on this Monday morning; we know that she wasn't asking anything of Heather at this point. Or perhaps Crystal just wanted to share this important event in order to receive from her teacher both a humane confirmation that this was an important event (which she did in Heather's "Ohhhhh") and a humane expression of empathy (as in Heather's "I'm sorry, Crystal"). Heather's joking about Crystal's book diminishes the book's importance and conversely elevates the importance of all of Crystal's other belongings, a move that, in its irreverence, establishes a human connection between Heather and Crystal. In her subsequent move to offer Crystal deadline changes as needed, Heather demonstrates empathy in a more teacher-ly way that helps provide a segue into her formal beginning of the day's class.

Equity-oriented teachers also can use a combination of empathy and humor to respond to students' expressions of frustration about their grade in the class. Such expressions of frustration can be difficult for teachers to respond to because they can feel like personal attacks. But, as in the example below, when teachers respond to students' concerns about their grades with empathy, specificity, and humor, they can preserve the positive, humane interpersonal relationships and sense of hopefulness both students and teachers need in order to position themselves positively toward retention. When the instance discussed below occurred, Melanie had just concluded one class, in which Antonio was a student, and as they talked, students from the next class began to enter the classroom. Here, Antonio, a Puerto Rican male, stays after class to ask Melanie about his grade.

Antonio initially walks toward the door, then makes a U-turn, arriving next to Melanie's desk as she sets up her computer's projection for her next class.

"Miss D, I need more points. I'm barely passing," Antonio complains.

"Okay. So I don't know all the stuff that we'll be doing up until the end of the marking period, but we have, I don't know, until the end of the month," Melanie thinks. "But, so, make sure, when we're doing work, you do your work and turn it in on time, all that stuff."

Antonio throws his head back in a large gesture of despair. "I need at least, like, eight, eight more percent. I need like—" He is interrupted by Melanie's laugh.

"—at least an 80—"

"That is a lot!" Melanie advises.

"—for my mom not to kill me." Antonio smiles weakly.

"So then you're gonna work for that 80, right," Melanie instructs. She then goes into great detail explaining which assignments are included in the interim grade report, when that report is being given to students, and what assignments are coming up. Students from the next class begin to enter the room.

"Why," he pauses for effect, "are you doing this?" He smiles.

"I told you guys last week! Where were you last week?"

"But I have a 72."

Melanie smiles and returns to the front of the room behind her desk. "Uh huh. And you're definitely capable of better than a 72."

"I know that."

"Yes. I know that, too." She makes eye contact with him. "So you're gonna work, right?"

Antonio sighs. "Sucks." He pounds on a student desk lightly several times, but he is still smiling. "So bad."

"It does," Melanie agrees, also still smiling. "Okay," she exhales. "Now where are you going? You're going to be late for class." She picks up a pass. Maya and other students enter the room.

"Math. In that class, I have an A in that class." He sports an even bigger smile as he chides her.

"Mm hmm. So why? It doesn't make *me* feel any way. It should make *you* feel *sad*! Where are you going; who's your math teacher?"

"Ms. Bartoll."

She begins writing the pass. "Okay."

He turns to Maya. "This sucks."

"Don't catch his attitude, Miss Davis," Maya warns enthusiastically.

Antonio retorts to Maya, "Don't catch *your* attitude in here. I'll set you down!" Maya and Antonio are standing face to face. Both are smiling.

"And you argue with people in my other classes, too?" Melanie observes. "You're just. Here you go." She hands Antonio the pass.

"Get out my classroom," Maya commands as she lightly pushes the back of Antonio's backpack toward the door.

"Bye, Antonio; you need to go to class so you're not late. Or too late." Melanie looks at the clock as he exits.

In this interaction (the conclusion of which also includes some 9th-grade-style flirting between Antonio and Maya!), Melanie responds extensively and specifically to Antonio's concern about his grade. Their light-hearted tone is suggested when Antonio throws his head back, a nonverbal gesture that I interpret as exasperation at hearing something he was afraid Melanie would say, but then clearly established in Antonio's,

"Why are you doing this?" and Melanie's, "Where were you last week?" and confirmed in their smiles. The fact that both a student and a teacher could smile during a conversation about the student's near-failing grade is surprising; it hints that while both were truly concerned, they were not unduly concerned, and that they had already established a strong relationship. At this point in the year, Antonio's grade of 72 was only 3 points from failing (70 was a D; 69 an F), yet he was never a student Melanie mentioned to me as "falling through the cracks."

Instead, as both of them agree during this interaction, he is "definitely capable of better than a 72," words that function both to express Melanie's confidence in him and to empathize with his predicament. Melanie treats Antonio's inquiry seriously, offering him some general advice ("do your work and turn it in on time") and some specific advice ("you have to get at least a B on that [portfolio] paper"). But she also uses light humor when she resists Antonio's indirect accusation that his grade in English is her fault and when she jokes about him arguing with people in her other classes. Even though Antonio and Melanie reference his math class and her other students as points of contrast in this interaction, they position Antonio as being valued and promising. Particularly because Antonio is a male student of color, Melanie's positive words about him demonstrate one important way that teachers can create a pull-in culture and influence students' positive positioning toward retention, a way that is discussed further in the section below. Additionally, because these references are made in humor at the end of a conversation about the more serious topic of Antonio's grade, they help create an upbeat conclusion and perhaps even a sense of hopefulness for Antonio as he leaves Melanie's classroom.

Position Students and Teachers as Members of a Shared Community

The third move that teachers committed to social justice can use between classes to create humanizing connections with their students involves cultivating a sense of the class period and/or the school as a community by using language that positions both students and teachers as members of this community. This move, already referenced in examples previously discussed in this chapter, is humanizing in nature because it places students and teachers on equal footing, as equal participants in a shared social group. Perhaps more than any of the others, this move can explicitly help create the sense of belonging that is so important in fostering a positive positioning toward retention.

In observing the teachers, I noticed that a distinguishing feature of this move is the teachers' repeated use of the first-person plural pronouns *we*, *our*, and *us*. While pronoun usage may seem like a trivial aspect of language, research has shown it to be incredibly powerful and consequential, albeit one of many factors influencing social interactions. For example, in his

extensive work on how patterns of pronoun usage function in social interactions, Wortham (1996) finds that the pronoun *we* "can both refer to and
establish an interactional group" (p. 332). Because speakers use pronouns
to create what Van De Mieroop (2015) calls "collective identities" and construct in-groups and out-groups, they are useful for understanding and analyzing the ways in which teachers and students think about the classroom
or school community. In the following simple but representative example,
Jasmine's language shows how pronouns can function this way in a brief
after-class interaction with Isaiah, who is sitting, backpack on, in a chair
next to the doorway after all of the other students have exited the room.

"Isaiah, what can I do for you?" Jasmine asks as she approaches him from
the middle of the room.
Isaiah just shakes his head.
"Nothing?" Jasmine checks.
"I'm staying for the game, plus the hallway's packed right now," he replies.
Jasmine laughs. "Who's, who's playing?"
Isaiah shrugs.
"You just know it's a game?"
"The freshmen's playing," Isaiah offers.
"You don't know, you don't know who we're playing today?" Jasmine
grins.
"I think, um, Heights."
"Oh, okay. Alrighty."
"We're gonna lose," Isaiah predicts.
"No, don't say that."
Isaiah starts to get up from the chair and walk to the door as Jasmine
turns and starts walking toward her desk, contradicting him. "We will win!"
"We lose, like, every game," he protests.
"Tiger pride!" Jasmine exclaims. Isaiah laughs, then exits the room.

This kind of interchange about sports might seem so common, so natural, as to be unremarkable. But it represents a pattern I have witnessed often
in equity-oriented teachers' practice, particularly in between-classes timespaces. In this instance, Jasmine alters the language of the conversation ever
so slightly from Isaiah's focus on "the freshmen" toward an inclusive "we,"
as in, "You don't know who *we're* playing today?" and "*We* will win!" as
opposed to alternatives like, "You don't know who *they're* playing today"
and "*They* will win!" Interestingly, Isaiah, an African American male, picks
up Jasmine's "we" usage in his "*We* lose, like, every game." The pattern
is observable also in Jasmine and Eleesha's conversation, discussed earlier
in the chapter, when Jasmine advises, "*We* have a talent show coming up
in April." Any uptake of these pronouns can indicate that the students are
ratifying the teacher's suggestions of a shared culture.

Like all teachers, equity-oriented teachers experience frustration when their plans go awry, and in response to such frustration, they often use a humor-infused variation of the move to cultivate a sense of the class period and/or the school as a community. As described in Chapter 3, the use of humor is a move equity-oriented teachers make in response to moments of crisis during class time. Through their use of humor, teachers also can build community as they respond to people or situations that they find frustrating. One representative exchange from Veronica's practice illustrates how this can happen. For months, she had been asking Diego, a Hispanic 9th-grade male, to stop talking, pay attention, keep his thoughts to himself, be quiet, and get in or stay in his seat (as in the vignette that opened Chapter 1). Among the strategies she tried using were talking one-on-one with him, talking with his parents, moving his seat to the side of the room for group-work, and moving his seat to the hallway during independent work time. By late February, Diego had, good-naturedly and enthusiastically, proceeded to talk during the class, and Veronica pursued another strategy: On a Thursday in late February, she laughingly bet Diego that he couldn't stay quiet for the rest of the marking period. The other students joined her in the bet with Diego, who had accepted the challenge. There was a snow day on Friday, and the transcription below captures the class's first moments together on Monday morning.

The bell rings to begin class. Veronica enters the classroom from the hallway, motions to Diego's empty student seat, turns one palm upward, and mouths, "Where's Diego?" to the students who are seated at their desks.

"He's absent today," Taiye answers.

Veronica furrows her brow. "Whyyyyyy?" she cries in disappointment.

Jametta expresses concern. "Miss J, he's not here today?"

Veronica starts walking to her desk and addresses the whole class. "You guys, do not remind Diego that we made a deal. Do not bring it up in conversation. Do you understand?"

"Bring what up?" Keesha asks.

"He has to fail. Or else we owe him money!" Veronica laughs. It gets loud. Many students are laughing and talking.

Tommy's voice rises above the others. "Wait, wait, wait, I'll give him five dollars."

"Let's give him five dollars so he can be quiet," DJ suggests.

"No no no no no," Veronica responds. "We want him to fail. Then he can be quiet. All right, let's catch up since we missed a day."

I can assure you, dear reader, with 99% confidence, that Veronica's teacher preparation program did not encourage her to engage in betting with her students or to say things like, "We want him to fail." However, as unconventional as these moves certainly are, and as ironic as it is that they position the rest of the class against one of its members, they operate in this particular timespace to both reveal and create a sense of community and a positive positioning toward retention, in part through the shared use of "we" and "us" (as in the contraction "Let's"). While the conversation reveals that some of the students, like Tommy and DJ, either misunderstood the bet or wanted to proceed in a different fashion than they agreed upon, it is clear that all participants in the conversation agree upon the goal of getting Diego to "be quiet," a phrase simultaneously initiated by DJ and Tommy and then ratified by Veronica. For his part, Diego experienced the bet as a community-building experience as well, seeming to enjoy the attention of his class; to no one's surprise, he lost the bet and, undeterred, happily continued talking nonstop to his classmates. As one of the happiest, most exuberant students I have ever met, Diego was a fitting subject for a move like this. The presence of smiling and laughing around this shared experience, crafted from the teacher's knowledge of the unique personalities in her classroom, suggests a solidified and solidifying sense of belonging for both Veronica and the students in this class.

Veronica's humorous "we"-ing move in this example, and the shared community that it represents, demonstrates the symbiotic relationship of student retention and teacher retention: As interdependent phenomena, the realities of one affect the other deeply. When equity-oriented teachers take it upon themselves to personally attend to the needs of students who are orienting negatively toward retention, their own positioning toward retention will shift. Whether it shifts negatively or positively depends on both their perceived sense of success in meeting students' needs and their perceived sense of having contributed to building the kind of positive community to which they seek to belong. Christensen (2010) explains that teachers need to be cognizant of the classroom culture they are creating because it shapes not only students' experiences in the short term but teachers' own experiences in the long term. She urges teachers to "work with students in such a way . . . that we want to stay in the classroom. . . . It has to be a place where we are getting something back out of it."

This "getting something back out of it" is a woefully under-discussed topic, as there is a powerful social pressure on teachers to act and think of themselves in conformity with the myth that they somehow are purely selfless beings with supernatural reserves of time, patience, and helpfulness. While it may seem shocking that teachers, too, need to derive satisfaction from their teaching practice, this is a critical fact often missed in discussions of teacher retention. The realities of high teacher attrition compel us, however, to pay more attention to the ways in which the classroom can be made a more satisfying place in which to work. In contrast to the current "reform" environment that has dehumanized education and chased so many qualified people away from the profession, I suggest that increased attention to the human aspects of teaching and learning, to the humanization of teaching and learning, to the cultivation of teacher/student relationships, is, in large sum, what is needed both to make classrooms places in which people want to spend time and to increase student and teacher retention as an act of social justice. As described above, the justice-oriented English teachers in this book consistently harnessed the unique potential of between-class time-spaces to accomplish these goals, making distinct sociolinguistic moves that tethered themselves and their students to one another and to their school.

EXAMINING THE PROMINENCE OF THE PROCEDURAL WITH STUDENTS WHO FAILED ENGLISH

My observations of before- and after-class interactions also suggest two extremely important and extremely uneasy truths, however. First, social conversations like all of those discussed above—in which the teachers and students made and deepened their connections to one another between classes—almost exclusively included students who went on to pass English. Put another way, humanizing, social teacher/student conversations between classes were *almost nonexistent* among students who went on to fail English for the year. Antonio, Eleesha, Isaiah, Keesha, Robyn, Thalma, and Tommy were non-focal students; and Crystal, Diego, Gwen, and Terrence were focal students who passed English—again, all of the students mentioned so far in this chapter passed English for the year. While it is impossible to know whether these social interactions somehow helped the students pass English and/or whether, in the other causal direction, being successful in English class made them more likely to interact socially with their teacher, the close relationship between passing English and being regularly involved in social teacher/student interactions is noteworthy. In this section, I discuss another noteworthy relationship: that of failing English and *not* being involved in humanizing between-class interactions with the teacher. Students who went on to fail English for the year were not regularly involved in such interactions with their teacher and thus were not likely to experience the kinds of connection and affirmation evident in the above examples.

But the absence of humanizing, between-class social interactions does not translate into a complete absence of before- and after-class interactions between students who went on to fail and their teachers. Instead, I observed that a more negative relationship—a relationship built on negatives—developed over time and led to fixed conversational patterns, identities, and results. Students in this group also did not appear to be involved in easily identifiable extracurricular activities that would make easy conversation starters for their teachers, and although their teachers had identified them as focal students, they often entered and left the classroom under the teachers' radar. This brings us to the second uneasy truth: Among the students who failed English, before- and after-class interactions with their teacher were characterized by a *prominence of the procedural*. This attention to the procedural consisted of a nearly singular focus on details (people, places, schedules/deadlines) and materials (pens/pencils, paper/journals, books, computers, and other technology).

Task-Oriented, Panic-Tinged Timespaces

I was surprised to find that the students who went on to fail English actually initiated before-class literacy interactions with the teacher much more frequently than any other group of students did. In this way, this group of students often sets the tone for their interactions with their teacher before class begins, and together, over time, these teacher/student pairs create task-oriented, panic-tinged timespaces—along with task-oriented, panic-tinged identities—in which students, in a somewhat agitated state, focus solely on the completion of short-term tasks. To illustrate this phenomenon, which I observed in all of the schools, I include and then discuss Melanie's interactions with Cordell, an African American male who had, at this time in the marking period, a 60% average, well below the lowest passing grade of 70%. Below, I share the entirety of their before-class talk over 2-week intervals to illustrate the consistency of patterns over time. Because several other students are involved in these interactions, the verbal interactions between Cordell and Melanie appear in bold type in order to make it easier to follow their one-on-one talk over time.

> Among the students who failed English, before- and after-class interactions with their teacher were characterized by a *prominence of the procedural*, a nearly singular focus on details (people, places, schedules/deadlines) and materials (pens/pencils, paper/journals, books, computers, and other technology).

March 12

Melanie is standing behind her desk, sorting papers as students are entering the room. Cordell is sitting at his desk. About half the students are present so far.

From his desk, Cordell calls, **"Do we turn this in to you? Right now? Miss Davis?"**

"What are you turning in?" Melanie asks.

"Uh." Cordell isn't sure how to respond.

In the meantime, Ashanti asks Melanie, "Do you always wear heels?"

"No, I didn't have on heels yesterday," Melanie reflects. "But I didn't see you yest—Well, I saw you yesterday!" The bell rings; the rest of the students enter the room. She sees Maya and addresses her. "Hold on to this." She walks across the front of the room and hands her a paper.

Cordell gets up and walks up to Melanie's desk and holds up a piece of paper in front of her. **"You want this?"** he asks again.

"No. What's that? The name thing? Hold on to it," she responds. He turns around and walks back to his desk with his paper. She looks around at the whole class. "All right, so if you can come in and take a seat, I have things to give back to you."

March 26

Melanie is hunched over behind her desk, surrounded by three female students—Rosa and Keyonnah, who need her help retrieving their presentation files, and Ashanti, who wants to tell Melanie about her plans for next year. Melanie is writing a pass for Keyonnah to go to the computer lab so that she can save her file in the right location. The bell rings.

"So click 'Save As,' then 'Student Pubs,' then look for the folder with my name on it," Melanie explains.

"Okay." Keyonnah nods.

"Miss Davis?" Ashanti requests.

At the same time, Rosa asks, "Uh, is she going up to the computer lab? Can I go? Because I can't edit it."

Also at the same time, Cordell appears in front of Melanie's desk and holds a paper up in front of her.

Ashanti shushes the whole class: "Shhhhhhh!"

"Because my—" Rosa tries again.

Cordell inserts, **"Here you go, Miss Davis."**

"Hmm? What's that?" Melanie responds.

"It's the uh, the uh," he points to the whiteboard. **"Definitions?"**

Melanie looks over his paper. **"Okay, I can look at that and tell that you still need help, so hold on."** Then, to the whole class, she raises her voice. "Okay, can you please take a seat?" She gives the pass to Keyonnah. Cordell returns to his desk with his paper, Keyonnah and Rosa leave the room, and the other students sit down.

April 16

Melanie is walking around to the students' desks, placing students' folders on their desks; some students are still entering the room. Cordell is sitting at his desk; the last student enters the room.

"Do we got an essay to do today, Miss Davis?" he inquires.

"You're what?" She didn't hear him.

"Do we got an essay to do today?" he repeats.

Melanie leans down to retrieve Cordell's essay from the basket under his desk and hands it to him as she talks. **"Yep, and you left yours here, so."**

"**It's due today?**" Cordell asks with widening eyes.
"**No, it's due on Thursday,**" Melanie reassures.
"**Oh.**"
Melanie walks to the front of the room. The bell rings, and she address-
es the whole class. "**All right, so come in, take a seat.**"

These brief interactions with a teacher, all initiated by Cordell before
class, illustrate the transactive timespace that can characterize before-class
interactions involving students who are struggling to pass English. By
"transactive," I mean that Cordell and Melanie's interactions in these moments consist primarily of exchanging details and materials, the prominence
of the procedural mentioned earlier. One noteworthy characteristic of the
above three interactions, and consistent with the many others they represent, is that they were Cordell and Melanie's first words of the day to each
other; they exchanged no personal or welcoming words beforehand—or af-
terward, for that matter.

The absence of humane discourse can serve as a manifestation of pushout culture, described in Chapter 1, in which a negative, impersonal, and
stressful climate prevails in a school—usually, an under-resourced school
and one serving students disproportionately affected by poverty. Such was
the case here, as the state had placed the school, as described in Chapter 2,
under unconscionable pressure to raise student test scores or face extreme
consequences. While typically people do not consciously try to make themselves feel unwelcome in any space, it is possible that through their language, which becomes normalized through repeated use, both teachers and
students unwittingly can become reproducers of pushout culture.

Further, although a fuller discussion of this point is beyond the scope
of this book, this brief example also shows how market-based school policies shape teachers' and students' language and focus in a disciplinary direction, and their sometimes-fearful preoccupation becomes avoiding the
discipline or punishment that will follow if they do not meet expectations.
When market-based policies use rhetoric that positions educational spaces
as primarily impersonal and data-oriented, other purposes of schooling are
pushed aside, notably those fostering the creation of a humane, creative,
critical, and democratic society (DeStigter, 2015; Sleeter, 2008). The sole
before-class focus on submitting a product by a deadline, which I observed
among Cordell and the other students who were failing English, provides
a glimpse into the inestimable ways that the misguided "accountability"
movement, or as critics call it, the "test and punish" movement, does not
indifferently or harmlessly measure teaching and learning from afar; rather, it distorts every aspect of education, right down to 5-second teacher/
student interactions before class. This is, as Cordell's example illustrates,
particularly true in under-resourced schools and among students who are
exhibiting signs of a negative positioning toward retention.

Active But Dissatisfying Interactions

The before-class interactions between Cordell and Melanie also demonstrate that students who are struggling to pass are generally not passive in the classroom. On the contrary, Cordell, for example, consistently arrived in the classroom with a great deal of energy and focus and inquired regularly about the details of English class. What is uncomfortable to notice is the pattern that developed between him and Melanie when he did so. First, she would not immediately understand what he said or meant (her first words to him were, "What are you turning in?" "What's that?" and "You're what?"). Her pattern of answering his question with another question required Cordell to repeat himself, which likely took some of the wind out of his—and Melanie's—sails. Her questioning mimics Cordell's, building on his panic rather than diffusing it. Second, in two of the three examples, or possibly even in all three, Cordell tried to submit work, and Melanie did not take it. In the first example, she told him to "hold on to" "the name thing"; in the second, she told him that he "still need[s] help" on "the definitions" and to "hold on." In the third, he expressed confusion about due dates; he had left an essay on his desk the day before and thought it was due, when in fact the present class period would be devoted to working on it.

Although it is important to note that these were only their initial interactions on these 3 days and that they did go on to discuss Cordell's next steps during class time, Melanie provided no immediate resolution for Cordell in the before-class timespace, and he left these initial interactions without knowing exactly what to do. Here, Cordell's identity as a student who is trying but is unsuccessful or unfinished, and Melanie's identity as a busy teacher with further instructions for which he will have to wait, were revealed and created. On each occasion, the material object of Cordell's work appeared physically between them, again suggestive of the transactive timespace they had created. Each of the three occasions ended with Cordell holding his (unfinished) work and Melanie walking away, a powerful image that encapsulates the unsatisfying, unsuccessful, unfinished nature of before-class teacher/student interactions involving students who went on to fail English.

The contrast represented by Melanie's between-class interaction with Cordell and her interaction with Antonio, discussed earlier in the chapter, is unsettling. It illustrates how one teacher's interactions with two students in similar academic situations (Cordell had a 60% average in English; Antonio a 72%) can reflect and help create very different positionings toward retention. While students who eventually went on to pass English, like Antonio, often performed successful and agentive identities in between-class teacher interactions, those who eventually went on to fail English, like Cordell, did not seem to experience the same sense of success, agency, humanity, or belonging in these timespaces. The teacher's identity formation in these contrasting interactions differed substantially as well: In her interaction with Antonio, Melanie created and revealed humane connection-making, a form of professional success from which she surely derived encouragement, but in her interaction with Cordell, Melanie created and revealed frustration and deferment, from which she likely derived dissatisfaction. In their before-class interactions, neither Melanie nor Cordell created a desirable timespace or community to which they would seek to belong, yet the opposite was true of Melanie and Antonio's before-class interactions.

What sense can we make, then, of the fact that, consistently across 2 years and four different schools, four new, equity-oriented teachers participated between classes in the creation of transactive timespaces with students who were on their radar as "falling through the cracks"? How can their commitment to teaching for social justice be read in their outside-of-class interactions with this group of students? Particularly with regard to before-class time, one important answer might lie in the balance that teachers need to maintain between starting class (proceeding with the lesson that they planned to benefit all students) and meeting the needs of individual students (improvising in response to individual students' questions as they enter the room). This is a tension that all teachers experience, before every class period, no matter what grade level they teach or how many years of experience they have; however, for equity-oriented teachers who are personally committed to helping those who are struggling, this tension is exacerbated. As a teacher and as a researcher, I have experienced this tension, the aforementioned tinges of panic, during before- and after-class interactions with students who were failing English; this panic is created by a desire to make the most of every second when a student who's been absent, is behind, or is failing, is present in the classroom. Because students who are failing are also absent frequently, the fleeting before- and after-class moments with them take on heightened importance for teachers committed to social justice. Ironically, equity-oriented teachers' desire to get a student quickly caught up, or get class started quickly so that individual interactions with failing students can occur during class time, also can result in a cessation of human connection and of a sense of belonging in school.

Another inescapable answer, briefly mentioned earlier, is the unwelcome intrusion of high-stakes testing, which disproportionately affects students of color and students in poverty, as well as their teachers, all of whom are threatened with teacher firings and school closings when "benchmarks" are not "met." The tinge of panic evident in Melanie and Cordell's before-class interactions reflects the panic landslide under which their school was struggling to survive. It will come as no surprise to equity-oriented readers that the level of panic I witnessed in teacher/student interactions was directly proportional to the school's percentage of students of color and low-income students; fewer transactive interactions were present in Jasmine's and Veronica's schools, and still fewer were evident in Heather's.

CONCLUSION: OVERCOMING BUSYNESS
TO CONNECT WITH STUDENTS BETWEEN CLASSES

As this chapter has shown, the busy moments between classes provide critical opportunities for equity-oriented teachers to impact individual students during one-on-one interactions in ways that they cannot during class time. When teachers engage in equity-oriented pedagogy before and after the bell, both they and their students cultivate a positive orientation toward school retention, a sense of connection to one another and to the setting in which they are connecting. It is, however, extremely easy for teachers to miss these possible ways to create a pull-in culture. Teachers typically are not taught to think about before-class or after-class timespaces as particularly instructive or important, if they are taught to think about them at all. Unless they resolve to proceed otherwise, many new English teachers—even those who enter the profession committed to working for social justice—likely will bend under the pressure of their numerous responsibilities and will always be either engaged in the task at hand or preparing for the next. In doing so, they will miss the opportunity to be fully present with their students, to engage in relationship-building with them outside of class time. I urge teachers to go well beyond the conventional wisdom of merely standing at the door and greeting students personally as they enter the room. Although doing so can be a solid point of entrée, I suggest that teachers create and follow concrete plans to connect deliberately and individually, before or after class, with students who are falling through the cracks, particularly those who have failing grades. Like other forms of pedagogy, making between-class connections requires a combination of commitment, preparation, and improvisation: committing to seek out a particular student, planning ahead to make themselves available to that specific student in a specific time and place, and improvising their responses to the student in that moment of interaction. Below, I provide equity-oriented teachers suggestions for overcoming common obstacles of busyness in order to carry out their commitment to connect with their most struggling students.

Obstacle #1: Learning the Ropes

It is especially easy for new teachers to miss these possibilities since, in addition to the above responsibilities, they spend a great deal of time "learning the ropes." They are still learning their responsibilities (e.g., curricula, standards, and assessment requirements); creating new instructional materials (e.g., unit and lesson plans, projects, handouts, activities, and rubrics); designing templates (e.g., teacher websites, course syllabi, parent newsletters, learning management system interfaces); and getting to know the school culture (e.g., what the student discipline policies are, and which colleague can help with what issue). They also are learning to maintain a work/life balance and are investing time in getting to know their colleagues and establishing groups of friends.

In order to overcome this obstacle as a new teacher, I suggest that you:

- Engage actively with your assigned mentor, or if you have not been assigned a mentor, either seek one out for yourself or ask an administrator to suggest one for you. You may even consider seeking out different mentors for different purposes (e.g., one for departmental issues, one for work/life balance, one for technology), rather than relying on one person to be your everything (Rockquemore, 2014). Get in the habit of writing down your questions, whenever you think of them, so that you can draw on this record when you have a chance to talk with your mentor(s).
- Immediately begin practicing a work/life balance and maintaining boundaries outside of school hours in a way that is healthful for you. For example, check and return email as infrequently as possible after school and over the weekend and/or on a set schedule so that you can start each week and each day refreshed to meet your students' needs. Begin or maintain healthy sleep, diet, and exercise regimens, and engage regularly in at least one hobby that fills your soul with joy. As a teacher, you must take care of yourself in order to take care of your students over the long term.
- Practice saying "No" or "Not yet," even and especially to yourself. Let go of your expectations of immediate perfection. While it is wonderful and understandable that you are excited to try everything you've been looking forward to trying as a teacher, give yourself permission to add these "extras" to your professional practice gradually. You likely have amazing ideas for bulletin boards, parent newsletters, podcasts, or teacher websites; you may receive invitations to become a coach, serve as a class advisor, or coordinate a major event, such as Homecoming. Say "No" or "Not this year." Many teachers are used to being both extra-prepared and people-pleasing, and so saying these words may require practice, but it gets easier, and it demonstrates that you are prioritizing your relationships with students, your students' success, and your own longevity in the field above all else.

Obstacle #2: Attending to Endless Details

Many teachers keep a subconscious between-classes To Do list with which they attend to the many details of teaching that cannot be accomplished during class time. These do not include the most time-intensive tasks of teaching—planning lessons, evaluating student work, and participating in meetings. Instead, these details include setting up technology or seating arrangements for the next class; dealing endlessly with technology issues (e.g., fixing or reporting the wi-fi or the projector that is not working, uploading documents in learning management systems, or scheduling student computer time); inputting grades; contacting or responding to communication from parents; completing administrative forms and reports; keeping track of which students have submitted which work in which stage of completion; responding to student absences that have already occurred and planning for upcoming student absences—including the formidable scheduling of make-up work; and juggling a frequently changing school schedule due to testing, assemblies, fieldtrips, and weather-related closings. To overcome this obstacle as a teacher, I suggest that you:

- Arrive early to get set up for the day, ideally before students arrive, in order to free yourself from other responsibilities between classes so that you can interact with students.
- Ask students to serve as class helpers or teacher's assistants. Delegate some responsibilities—such as moving students' seats or handing out materials—to these students while you are out in the hallway.
- Ask trusted colleagues whether they are willing to share their strategies for managing student absences and make-up tests, from having a folder for unclaimed returned work in each class to posting a sign-up sheet or online calendar for students to schedule their own make-up quizzes or tests.
- Ask trusted colleagues whether they are willing to share templates for common student and parent email communications that you can personalize, such as those expressing concern over student grades or requesting a conference. You aren't the first teacher ever to write such an email; there's no need to reinvent the wheel!
- Never be afraid to ask for help. As a new teacher, you may experience some degree of newness fatigue, when you feel like you have to ask for help on just about everything, but don't give in to that feeling. If you have tried repeatedly to do or to fix something yourself without success, ask. Don't suffer in silence or avoid using technology that is frustrating you. Your colleagues expect you to ask for help; they will help you, just as you will return the favor both to them and to other novices in a situation when you are the one with more experience.

Obstacle #3: Responding to Student Work

For English teachers, the extra pressure generated by nearly constant piles of papers to grade cannot be overstated. (For the uninitiated, if an English teacher assigns a 2-page paper to five 20-student classes, there will be a total of 200 pages of writing to read. If 15 minutes were spent reading and responding to each of the 100 students' papers, this task would require 25 hours outside of class time to complete.) Recognizing how this pressure can play out during the school day is essential to understanding the reality of the daily professional life of English teachers. For this particular group of teachers, every second counts, and, importantly, every task not accomplished during the day piles up for their attention during after-school hours, when they have already worked 8 or more hours. English teachers' To Do list, in particular, threatens to fill every crevice of their professional and personal lives, including the moments between classes.

I suggest that, to overcome this obstacle as an English teacher, you:

- Regularly set aside time for students to draft and workshop their writing during class time, when you can help students get started, respond to questions, notice and address common difficulties, and offer encouragement in person. This time often increases the quality of students' work and therefore can reduce your grading time.

- Set and stick to a time limit for grading each paper, using a timer to keep track.

- Train yourself to use restraint. Don't mark every instance of every grammar, usage, or spelling error in a student's paper. Mark one example of a pattern, note that this is a pattern you are noticing, and direct the student to talk with you and/or consult a classroom resource to address the error.

- Use rubrics to focus your attention. Don't grade every aspect of student writing in every assignment.

- Keep track of common errors students are making in each assignment so that you can avoid writing the same comments over and over. Instead, teach a mini-lesson on each common error, ask students to revise their work based on the mini-lesson, and make note in your lesson plans that these mini-lesson(s) should precede the due date next time.

- Whenever you can, spread out major paper due dates so that you have only one set of papers to grade at a time, and work around major events in your personal life.

- Consider rolling submissions of larger student projects so that you are, for example, bringing home only five research papers a day over 10 days instead of bringing home 50 research papers at once. Students could sign up for one of the 10 due dates that best fits their own schedule.

QUESTIONS FOR TEACHER REFLECTION, DISCUSSION, AND ACTION

1. Do I welcome all of my students individually on most days? Which students do I routinely miss welcoming, and what do I need to do differently to make them feel welcome in my classroom?

2. How available am I to talk, unfettered, with my students in the moments immediately before class starts and after class ends? If this is a challenge for me, what can I do differently to open up this timespace as a way to demonstrate my commitment to equity?

   a. What tasks need to be done to set up for class (e.g., distributing materials, moving furniture, setting up technology)? Can I arrive in the classroom earlier to get set up for class? Can I simplify the set-up necessary to get students started with classwork as they enter, or create more structured routines? Can I arrange for student volunteers (particularly those who routinely arrive to class early) to take charge of routine tasks?

   b. Where can I position myself physically in an in-between space, such as the hallway or back or side of the classroom, to provide students with a visual signal that a different kind of talk is possible?

   c. When would it be helpful for me to end class a few minutes early to create time for one-on-one talk? With which student(s)?

3. What artifacts are already part of my classroom décor that I can use to initiate conversation with my students? Or what artifacts could I display in my classroom in order to serve this function?

4. Using this chapter's lens on between-class periods, what positionings toward retention have I been facilitating with my students during these unique timespaces? How have I positioned myself and/or my students as members of a shared classroom or school community, and in what specific ways can I do more of this? With which students? Do I ever use pronouns like *we* and *us* to help create a sense of community?

5. How can I diminish "the prominence of the procedural" in my between-class dialogue with students who are failing to make room for creating more humane connections? To cut down on procedural student questions:

   a. How can I post or share my agenda, due dates, materials needed, and other information more regularly or effectively?

   b. How can I streamline student processes or procedures, such as visiting the bathroom or locker, borrowing pencils or pens, retrieving missed work, and scheduling make-up work or extra help? Can students take care of these details without me? If not, what can I change?

CHAPTER 5

Staying to Talk with Students Who Are Falling Through the Cracks

We will never develop some ideal instructional program that can be exported from classroom to classroom. In the end, programs that come out of boxes do not work. Great teaching will always be about relationships, and programs do not build relationships; people do. (Duncan-Andrade, 2007, p. 636)

While the previous chapter focused on organic teacher/student interactions that arise naturally and publicly as the teacher and students negotiate the chaos of changing classes, this chapter focuses on a very different kind of teacher/student interaction that can occur between classes: when a teacher invites an individual focal student to meet after class and they then stay to talk privately in the classroom together. In contrast to the interactions described in Chapter 4, these staying-to-talk interactions are not organic; instead, they are intentional, strategic practices that I observed equity-oriented teachers initiate in order to reach out to and try to "catch" a student whom they perceived to be falling through the cracks. Staying-to-talk interactions represent a special category of focused intervention by equity-oriented teachers that is outside the scope of common teacher/student interactions.

Compared with all of the other interactions discussed so far in this book, not only those between classes but also during classes, these intentional staying-to-talk interactions with students were among the most powerful ways that I saw equity-oriented teachers try to connect with students about whose success they were concerned. When the teachers needed to problem-solve with a student who had a failing or near-failing grade in the class, with a student who experienced or caused some sort of difficulty during class time, or with a student whom they hadn't connected with in a while, they initiated private, after-class interactions with these individual students. In any kind of one-on-one interaction, teachers give students the gift of undivided attention and time in the midst of an otherwise chaotic school day. But staying-to-talk meetings represent a much more intense kind of interaction, given that they are initiated by teachers, that students have to endure the somewhat uncomfortable period between being invited to meet and actually meeting, and that they occur privately, once everyone else has vacated the classroom. Although students may experience invitations to these meetings with teachers as a sign that they are "in trouble" and thus approach them with a degree of apprehension, the meetings nevertheless can communicate that the teacher is paying attention to, or investing in, the student and signal to the student his or her value and sense of promise—interaction by-products that can increase student positioning toward retention. At the same time, teachers who initiate staying-to-talk meetings are engaging in a highly agentive act, making a move through which they experience agency, "the satisfying power to take meaningful action and see the results of our decisions and choices" (Murray, 1997, p. 381), another long-term predictor of teacher retention (e.g., Ingersoll, 2007).

During the course of my study, all of the students whom the teachers invited to stay to talk had failing or near-failing grades when they met after class but ultimately went on to pass English for the year. On the other hand, and similar to the patterns described in the previous chapter, I did not observe the teachers issue such invitations to any of the eight students who ultimately went on to fail English. Although correlation is not causation, these are significant findings that warrant a closer look at what kinds of talk actually occur in these staying-to-talk timespaces. What kinds of discursive moves do equity-oriented teachers make in staying-to-talk meetings with students with failing grades? What do these moves have to do with equity? And what identities and positioning toward retention do the teachers and students reveal and create during these meetings?

A STAYING-TO-TALK EXAMPLE

This chapter focuses on one extended staying-to-talk example because it provides an important window into answering these questions and enables us to witness what the phenomenon of private after-class interactions between new, equity-oriented teachers and students who are falling through the cracks "means as it is socially enacted within a particular case" (Dyson & Genishi, 2005, p. 10). This dialogue provides a contrast with the "prominence of the procedural" interactions described in the previous chapter by illustrating how a new, equity-oriented teacher used the staying-to-talk timespace to initiate a deeply meaningful, personalized interaction with a student about whose success she was concerned. The interaction illustrates all of the trends that I observed across the four teachers' private after-class meetings with focal students. Given that the after-class context represents relative freedom from fixed identities and language use, as well as from the sociocultural influences of other students in the room, it offers important affordances for examining how new, equity-oriented teachers and students with failing or near-failing grades use language to create and reveal both their identities with respect to one another and their positionings toward retention.

In my representation of this interaction, I indicate in bold type each of the "opening moves" (Eggins & Slade, 1997), which are speakers' attempts to take the conversation in a new direction and, as such, represent acts of agency and power as well as moments of negotiation. I also divide the conversation into discrete sections created by these opening moves (Gee, 1996; Wells, 1999; Wortham, 2001), a strategy I have found helpful in examining interactive positioning during difficult conversations between teachers and students (Bieler, 2010).

The immediate impetus for this particular staying-to-talk episode occurred about halfway through a class period in February, when Veronica arrived at the desk of Vishon, an African American male, during a notebook check, which she was conducting as the students were engaged in individual seatwork. Veronica arrived at Vishon's desk after having checked the notebooks of about half the class, grading them on whether all of the readings, teacher-generated materials, and student work were included and in the correct section. Vishon indicated that his notebook wasn't ready, and she asked, "Do you want me to just put zeroes in for you?" He responded with a quick, unapologetic yes, and when he offered no further discussion, she proceeded without comment to the next student. This 0/20 grade instantly and significantly dropped his cumulative English grade for the marking period into failing territory. While Vishon's work tended to be average to strong on the whole, this was the second time in a month that he had earned a zero on an easy assignment. And so, right before she dismissed the class at the end of the period, Veronica asked, "Vishon, can you stay after class for me?"

As most of the students left quickly, Veronica stayed seated atop a stool, and Vishon, backpack straps across both shoulders, took a seat atop a student desk across from her, kicking his feet back and forth. They spent a few awkward moments across from each other, waiting for the last two students to pack up and leave the room before they started talking, and Veronica filled the silence by asking the last student to pick up and bring her a paper she spied on the floor near his desk. Veronica began the private, after-class meeting with Vishon only when that last student finally disappeared into the hallway.

Section 1

Veronica breaks the silence. **"What's up with your I-don't-care attitude?"** She is looking directly at him.

"What do you mean?" Vishon asks, looking down, not at her.

"Ohhh, like you just accepted your zeroes today. You even requested them." She pauses briefly. "You're okay with turning in your work late."

"It was, my notebook's messed up. I woulda got a zero on it anyway."

"Why?"

"'Cause I don't care about it."

"That's, that's," she points a finger at him, "the I-don't-care attitude I'm making reference to. It's quite obvious. It's not like you're hiding it at all."

"Why would I, why would I hide—hide it?"

"Most people hide the fact that they don't care about their schoolwork; what's up with you? Hold on." She places their conversation on hold when other students enter the room for something, and she waits to resume until after the students leave. "When someone is blatantly just, 'Uh, I'm not gonna do it,' and I know they're capable, that concerns me." She is still looking at him, and he is still looking down.

Section 2

"How do you know I'm capable of doing my work?" Vishon asks.

"I do know you're capable, Vishon."

Sixteen uncomfortable seconds pass as they sit in silence.

Section 3

Veronica finally breaks the silence by humming, which causes Vishon to look up at her expectantly, smiling.

"I'm waiting for you to respond," Veronica offers.

"What am I supposed to say to that?" He exhales and looks back down.

Section 4

Veronica raises her shoulders. "You keep trying to pull off this 'I can't do it' or 'I'm not capable of it.' As an instructor, I know when kids are struggling because they can't read, they can't write, there's a learning disability. You don't have any of those issues. It's just straight up 'I'm lazy,' 'I don't want to do it,' 'I'm not gonna do it.' There's a difference. So what are you gonna do about this attitude?" She leans slightly toward him. "And this is me coming to you first before going to your parents and giving you the opportunity to fix whatever's going on, on your own."

Section 5

Vishon talks over the bell ringing to begin the next class. "But I'm confused because you're saying that you don't care." He looks up at her as he speaks, then looks back down when he finishes.

"Because I don't care, I'm not, like, I'm not gonna track down Rashed to turn in his assignment, even though I know he hasn't done it and he doesn't know when it's due. He should have turned it in when it was due. I'm not gonna chase him. However, your issue is just 'I just wanna be lazy,'" Veronica explains.

Section 6

She continues. "What classes are you trying to get into for next year?"

"I don't even want to be here." He looks up at her.

"So why don't you do what you need to do to get out?"

"My mom's making me stay."

"Okay, so you have to be here, you don't have a choice."

Vishon sighs and looks back down.

"So you need to make the best of it," Veronica advises. An 8-second pause follows.

Section 7

"You can sit here as long as you want, Vishon. I really don't care."

"What am I supposed to say?"

"You're supposed to say—"

"Am I supposed to give you an answer?"

Section 8

"Yeah!" Veronica replies. **"What do you wanna do to improve your attitude and improve your work in my classroom? Get it up to the caliber that I know it can and should be."**

Vishon blows air, making his lips vibrate, and turns slightly to his left.

"I know. This is so stressful," Veronica states.

Section 9

"The crazy thing, Vishon, is?" Veronica continues, **"I believe that most of the work we do here in this classroom,"** she motions toward the whiteboard, **"isn't that hard for you.** That you could do it. And it would not be that big of a problem for you. You may struggle with writing, because the topics don't interest you, or you don't know how to start, or something simple, of that sort. But for the most part, you know what you're doing." She starts tapping her pen on her leg.

Section 10

"I don't see how all you teachers think you all know this," Vishon appeals.

"Okay, am I wrong?" Veronica quickly rejoins.

"No."

"Oh, okay, so."

"I mean—"

"So my assessment is right." Veronica holds up her right palm toward him in a "Wait" movement.

Section 11

"You, you're capable," Veronica empathizes. **"You can do it. You just choose not to."**

Vishon shakes his head and quietly protests: "No."

Section 12

"This is me coming to you," Veronica explains. "Next time, I'm not going to you; I'm going to your parents. Do you understand?"

Vishon turns toward his right and looks at the floor. "I'm fine with that." (See Figure 5.1.)

"You don't have a problem with it, so I should go to them now because you're not gonna change anything anyway?" Veronica asks.

"I'm just gonna get in trouble," Vishon claims.

"Well, wouldn't you rather adjust it here in the classroom and never have to go home and hear your mom yell at you, 'cause you do, that's what you complain about, your mom's attitude, all the time? Why don't you fix it here so that I don't have to go to her?"

Section 13

"I just, I, I, I'm just confused, how, like you say you don't care about it. But like, me being lazy, I'm not affecting nobody else in the class. Like I was quiet today. I'm not affecting nobody else in the class but myself," Vishon asserts.

Section 14

Veronica replies gently, "Because I see potential and you're wasting it."

Vishon hangs his head lower and blows air out audibly through his lips.

Section 15

"Every, every teacher says that," Vishon says disapprovingly.

"I know. I know it's tough being hard, Vishon, I know." Veronica raises both her hands, palms up. "It's difficult. People have expectations from you. I do."

Figure 5.1. Staying to Talk

Section 16

She continues. "**If we need to, we can get a guidance counselor involved,** get your parents involved, we can have a big old sit-down, which I know you don't want—" Here, Vishon laughs lightly.

"—About what you do in my class, and in other classes," Veronica goes on. "I can start going to your other teachers, find out what you're doing in their class. We can make a big thing out of something that doesn't have to be big at all. If you'd like me to."

Section 17

"**But you say you don't care,**" Vishon replies again. "That's why I, why I act like this, 'cause you say you don't care, so I don't care either, so that's why I'm just gonna sleep or do whatever I do."

"Okay, if that's the attitude you want to take, like I said, we can blow this up. Or—"

"Why?" he asks, laughing a little more now.

"Because!" Veronica exclaims. "I just explained it to you. You're responsible for yourself. That's what I mean when I say I don't care. You're responsible for turning in your work on time, coming in with your materials ready, being prepared at all times. School is your job. When you go to work, you need to have all the necessities ready. I do care when I see a student who is bright and is just literally choosing to be lazy. That bothers me. Why? Because I have other students who work very hard and still struggle."

Section 18

"**You could be a model,** you could be an example in the classroom, you choose not to be," Veronica maintains.

Section 19

"**I'm not going to explain myself to you again.** You either come to my class tomorrow ready to work, being the bright, intelligent young man that you are, or I go to your parents. I told you from the beginning I'll come to you first before I go to your parents or before I go to guidance counselors. This is that conversation. After this, I'm not going to you anymore, Vishon. You adjust yourself, like a young adult, or I have to go talk to mommy and daddy. Okay?"

"Mm hmm," Vishon responds.

"Let's not make a habit of this. Nip it in the bud, get our lives together so we can live happily together, get back to bickering the way that we normally do." She pauses for a few seconds. "Does that sound like a plan?"

"Sure," Vishon replies quietly.

"You get your life together, and I don't have to go talk to your parents?" Veronica asks.

He lowers his head, crosses his arms, and rests his right cheek on his right hand, which is in a fist. "Sure," Vishon responds quietly, again.

"Appreciate it. Where are you going?"

"Math." They do not talk for a few seconds as she writes out his pass.

Veronica finishes, smiling, and fixes her eyes on him. "I look forward to seeing your peppy, energetic self tomorrow." She offers him the pass with a straight, outstretched right arm. He responds with a weak breathing-out laugh, takes the pass, and stands up.

"Have a great day, Vishon," she adds. He walks out wordlessly.

FOCUS ON STUDENT POTENTIAL AND THE NEED FOR CHANGE

This representative example of a staying-to-talk interaction illustrates how equity-oriented teachers use the after-class timespace both to express concern for and to lift up students. Another important way to read Veronica and Vishon's after-class conversation is as an extended negotiation of these two simultaneous areas of focus. In Section 1, Veronica immediately establishes a clear intent to focus the meeting on Vishon's "I-don't-care attitude," initially seeking an explanation from Vishon and then, in Section 8, shifting to ask explicitly about his plans to change. As many people do to avoid confrontations, Vishon persistently appears to try to shift the focus away from himself: In each of his six opening moves, his primary focus is either on Veronica or on his teachers as a whole, although as I describe below, these conversational moves have great significance. Paralleling Vishon's persistent attempts to focus on Veronica, she persistently attempts to focus on his potential—even to the point of doing so in the midst of a threat, as seen in Section 19!

Veronica's emphasis on Vishon's potential displays a common feature of social justice pedagogy: As Duncan-Andrade (2007) argues, equity-oriented teachers should have high expectations for their students and be "indignant about student failure" (p. 635), but they should also love and support students in ways that help them meet those expectations. Veronica provides an important model here, as she both responded thoughtfully to the student's questions and concerns but also firmly refocused the conversation on him each time. In his work, Duncan-Andrade emphasizes the foundational need for teachers, specifically urban teachers, to develop a relationship of trust with their students, and he advocates for teachers to actively support but "not coddle" students (p. 634). This snapshot of Veronica's practice illustrates what support can look and sound like in a one-on-one teacher/student interaction.

When Vishon does not provide a specific answer to Veronica's inquiry about what he would "do to improve . . . [his] attitude and . . . work" (Section 8), Veronica slowly escalates her language, culminating in a clear, unabashed threat that is truly indignant about student failure: "You either come to my class tomorrow ready to work, being the bright, intelligent young man that you are, or I go to your parents" (Section 19). In this and other after-class interactions with students who were struggling in her class, Veronica demonstrates a pattern of critiquing, providing encouragement, and then urging change. She balances critique, which was likely difficult for Vishon to hear, with abundant references to his capabilities. When teachers name the strengths of and give positive feedback to students who, like Vishon, are members of marginalized groups, they are creating a pull-in culture; they are helping to make school a positive place for students.

> The importance of teachers' skillful use of the after-class time-space to encourage and emphasize the potential of students who are struggling cannot be overstated because this academic struggle can co-occur as part of youth's larger negotiation of their identities and cultures.

Veronica's policy of meeting first with students in difficulty, before involving other adults, is one way for equity-oriented teachers to demonstrate that they respect their students. Her move in Section 6 to focus on helping the student meet his own goals also demonstrates a humanizing pedagogy. Particularly in instances like this, where a student is experiencing the frustration that can come from diminished agency (as suggested by his posture and as evident in his statement, "I don't even want to be here. My mom's making me stay"), teachers' one-on-one outreach can demonstrate a valuing of the individual that goes against the grain of pushout culture. In this way, the staying-to-talk timespace provides a nonthreatening microclimate that can build youth engagement with teachers and with schools. The importance of using the after-class timespace to encourage and emphasize the potential of students who are struggling cannot be overstated because, as I discuss below, this academic struggle can co-occur as part of youth's larger negotiation of their identities and cultures. This negotiation makes the private nature of staying-to-talk interactions particularly important for equity-oriented educators who are seeking to connect with students, as individuals, away from the immediate influence of others in their social sphere.

Grounding Interactions in Knowledge of a Student's Transaction with/in Culture(s)

Both Veronica's initiation of and use of language during this staying-to-talk interaction with Vishon were grounded in her specific knowledge about him as an individual and, in this way, provide a powerful demonstration of what culturally sustaining pedagogy (Paris, 2012; Paris & Alim, 2014) can look and sound like in one-on-one interactions between equity-oriented teachers and their students. While at first glance, some readers might question the way that Veronica characterizes Vishon's behavior, I argue that she skillfully and in culturally sustaining ways used what she knew about Vishon and his family to inform when, where, and how she interacted with him. For example, in one of our discussions about focal students during her prep period, Veronica noted that one of Vishon's parents recently had remarried, and she worried that he was not receiving much attention at home. But Veronica's holistic approach to Vishon was not limited to understanding his personal circumstances; it also was very much informed by her own circumstances. On a separate occasion, during her exit interview, which occurred about a month after the school year ended, Veronica shared that both growing up and as an adult, she has been motivated to succeed in part because of a sense of accountability to her grandparents. During a discussion about the strong relationship she sees between her students' achievement and their parents' involvement, Veronica used herself as a personal example of the role of elders' expectations in student motivation:

> Like for me, it was my grandparents who held really high expectations for me. If *they* didn't have high expectations for me, if I didn't know that when I went to [their city] and they asked me what I was doing in school, it had to be something positive, or I was *toast*. And that was what I kept in my mind when I didn't want to *do* stuff. I was like, "I'm not telling my Grandmom and Pop-pop that I'm not doing anything. They'll be so upset with me." You have to reinforce those things. Even now, I'm a grown adult and I still, I'm going to go see my grandparents today. And I still feel like I have to say, you know, I'm not sitting around doing nothing. I am doing *something*. Your kid should feel that way. That's, I feel like that's the biggest factor.

This excerpt from Veronica's exit interview powerfully reveals her belief that youth respond when elders hold them personally accountable for achieving success. She went on to discuss further how it was clear to her as a teacher which focal students had such elders in their lives and which did not. Veronica's narrative provides an important lens through which to view her staying-to-talk interaction with Vishon: It helps us see that Veronica understood Vishon to be currently experiencing diminished parental influence; knew elders' expectations to be extremely beneficial in her own life; and through a staying-to-talk interaction, assumed some aspects of this important elder role in order to provide for Vishon the same kind of positive uplift she herself has experienced.

In short, because this new teacher's staying-to-talk pedagogy is rooted in her deep knowledge of an individual student's needs and in her commitment to sustaining an aspect of his culture—and in fact their shared culture—it provides a powerful example of culturally sustaining pedagogy. Veronica's knowledge of elders' important role in the community and her resulting sociolinguistic performance as a surrogate elder figure for Vishon recall the kinds of teacher/student relationship described in many studies of culturally relevant pedagogy—from Ladson-Billings's (1994) notion that students and teachers often form a kind of "extended family" (p. 61) to Rolón-Dow's (2005) claim that when engaged in critical care praxis, educators "seek to transform race-conscious ideological and political orientations into pedagogical approaches" (p. 106).

However, as Paris and Alim (2014) note, there is a tension inherent in reading a single interaction like this as purely culturally sustaining in nature. They caution that "asset pedagogies too often draw overdeterministic links between race and language, literacy, and cultural practice" and urge equity-oriented teachers and scholars instead to "understand the ways young people are enacting race, ethnicity, language, literacy, and cultural practices in both traditional *and* evolving ways" (p. 90, emphasis in original). In other words, none of us should assume that just because we know or have experienced cultural practices that a student may hold as traditional—even when we share the same cultural background, as Veronica and Vishon do here—we must be open to the new, evolving ways that the student may be enacting culture. What if Vishon, for example, as Kirkland (2013) suggests in his work on young Black men, felt as if he were being constructed as "a problem," quoting Du Bois, or "resisted because [he was] being resisted" (p. 99)? I explore these possibilities in the next sections, focusing on how, in this staying-to-talk interaction, Veronica worked to influence Vishon as he navigated multiple aspects of his identity and culture.

Positioning Toward Retention in a Culture of Being or Acting "Hard"

The decision to hold staying-to-talk meetings within the after-class timespace can represent an additional demonstration of respect and, I argue, a critical act of equity pedagogy. This point becomes clear in Section 15, when Veronica works to comfort Vishon by saying, "I know. I know it's tough being hard, Vishon, I know. It's difficult. People have expectations from you. I do." This extremely important expression of empathy could never have occurred during the before-class or during-class timespaces and demonstrates the possibilities of staying to talk for students with failing grades. The term *hard* here may be significant; Rios (2006) describes it as "pretending to be bad in order to gain respect," one of many "strategies of survival in order to cope with the violence of the state and other institutions that criminalize and punish" Black and Latino male youth (p. 48). Rios goes on to discuss Willis's (1977) work, which concludes that, sadly, these strategies often further marginalize those who utilize them. Dance (2001) distinguishes between *being* hard ("a street-savvy and tough gangster who has actually committed criminal, violent, and ruthless acts") and *acting* hard (being a "hardcore wannabe," "because it is fashionable or prestigious, that is to say, a superficial means of gaining social esteem in urban youth culture, . . . [with] either no involvement or sporadic, peer-pressured involvement in the negative aspects of street culture") (p. 404).

That Veronica identifies Vishon with the term *hard* may demonstrate her knowledge of and respect for Vishon and his community (the people who "have expectations from you"), and she emphasizes her sincerity and empathy with a concluding, "I do." Insofar as *hard* also can be used synonymously with *tough* or *cold*, Veronica herself, interestingly, also can be read as appearing *hard* in this staying-to-talk instance; her tone, together with her saying "I know" three times, positions her as an ally, perhaps one with even more experience on the matter than she is divulging. Interestingly, Veronica doesn't spend time talking with Vishon specifically about his notebook (e.g., what was "messed up" about it, or why it was "messed up"); instead, she seems to regard these details as symptoms of a larger, more important issue that more urgently deserved their attention, recalling Jasmine's advice in Chapter 3. Veronica's decision not to talk with Vishon publicly during the notebook check during class, her invitation to talk with Vishon after class, her restraint in not talking with him until all other students had left the room: These are the moves of an equity-oriented educator who knows and respects the student and his community enough to hold him accountable while still protecting his reputation—or, perhaps enough to protect his reputation *in order to* hold him accountable.

It is natural to want to leave a place if we feel that our reputation is beyond our control, if the place's narrative about us contradicts the one we ourselves wish to author. This understanding is key to the idea that in their interactions, teachers and students are always forming and revealing their positioning toward retention. In the interaction discussed here, Veronica positions Vishon as someone who is wasting his potential (Section 14) and communicates her expectation that he start acting like "the bright, intelligent young man" that he is (Section 19), even though she knows "it's tough being hard" (Section 15). And it is perhaps this conflict—between acting hard and being successful in school—that makes this particular conversation, and all those it represents, so difficult and so critical. Essentially, Veronica is attempting to raise Vishon's awareness that he is acting in ways that are not aligned with school success, let Vishon know that she is confident in his ability to succeed in this place, and challenge him to begin orienting himself more positively toward school. While it may seem ironic that Veronica uses the third space of after-class time (as discussed in Chapter 4) to challenge a student to orient himself toward the first space (school), it is precisely what is needed when a student appears to be negatively orienting him- or herself toward staying in school.

For her part, Veronica's initiation and leading of this conversation demonstrate a strong positioning toward retention. In fact, I argue that because she performed her social justice commitments during this interaction, she not only demonstrated but also created a positive positioning toward retention as she interacted with Vishon. In this interaction, her words carry passion and power. The number of opening moves she made, the questions she addressed directly to Vishon, her long pauses, humming, and pen tapping all communicate her strong sense of agency: She was undeniably in charge of this meeting with this student. And, as we know from Ingersoll's (2002) research on teacher attrition, a low sense of teacher influence or control—teacher agency—is a major factor in teachers' job dissatisfaction and decisions to leave teaching. In another instance of a pattern discussed in Chapter 4, Veronica concluded this staying-to-talk interaction by using plural pronouns like *we* and *our* and by using humor-infused language to perform unity between herself and Vishon: "Let's not make a habit of this. Nip it in the bud, get **our** lives together so **we** can live happily together, get back to bickering the way that **we** normally do" (Section 19). In this move, Veronica demonstrates her continued valuing of this teacher/student relationship, one that clearly carries a history, and in so doing sets up a contrast between "this" kind of staying-to-talk meeting and "bickering the way that we normally do." Her humorous description of their relationship is forward-looking and simultaneously seems to call attention to the seriousness of their meeting, characterize it as an anomaly compared with their past and future "normal," and potentially assuage Vishon's worries. In Veronica's language, a strong sense of teacher agency is palpable: There is a sense that she as a teacher is steadfast and can effect change in an individual student's life, and this sense bodes well as an indicator of positive positioning toward retention.

Grading to Respect Being or Acting "Hard"

Looking across all of his grades for 9th-grade English with Veronica, it is clear that this after-class conversation did not change the pattern that Vishon had already begun to establish: He continued to earn strong grades in major assessments and projects—essays and tests that were completed privately during class time—and to earn zeroes on in-class work and home-work—work typically completed or submitted in view of others. With this pattern, Vishon successfully earned a respectable C in each marking period and in the class overall, a grade that also permitted his eligibility for sports and, in part, enabled his competitiveness for college admission and scholarships. What Vishon achieved was balance, a balance that enabled him to please both "every teacher" who saw his potential and "people" who, as Veronica observed, "[had] expectations from" him (Section 15). It enabled him to act "hard" by not doing or not submitting work in class when surrounded by his peers, thus maintaining a desirable identity at school—a key factor in maintaining a positive association with school. Such a balance was made possible by Veronica's grading structure, which, intentionally or not, gave equal weight to students' private work (undertaken and submitted privately to the teacher, like major assessments or individual projects) and public work (undertaken and submitted more publicly, such as seatwork or group projects). Veronica's grading structure helped Vishon preserve the plurality within himself, as he transacted with/in multiple past and present cultural norms. It raises the possibility of structuring course grade weights (e.g., the percentages of a marking period grade that come from in-class versus out-of-class work) as an act of social justice pedagogy. When their requirements are respectful of students as they navigate their identities and communities, teachers can increase opportunities for students to align their personal goals with scholastic goals and, in this way, can increase their students' chances of successfully reaching both.

Practicing Equity Pedagogy to Express "Caring" and Support for Youth Agency

Despite our very best intentions as social justice educators, we can be misunderstood, and our words and actions can cause students to respond in ways that we do not anticipate. Our intention in using a word or phrase may have precious little bearing on how it is received, particularly when our listeners' experiences with the word or phrase have led them toward alternative understandings. I reference this tension here because it can threaten to reduce equity-oriented teachers' effectiveness by lurking, unaddressed and unresolved, beneath the surface of teacher/student relationships. And it is the appearance of this tension—and its resolution—in Veronica and Vishon's conversation that leads us to the chapter's final point: While earlier, I emphasized the teacher's demonstration of agency, here I want to trace the ways that this teacher and student experienced tension around the expression "I don't care" in order to show how the after-class timespace also offers a unique and important opportunity to increase youth agency. Veronica and Vishon's staying-to-talk interaction makes explicit the central role that "caring" is assumed to play in equity-oriented pedagogy, particularly the ways in which race, ethnicity, and culture shape teachers' and students' experiences of caring (e.g., Irizarry, 2007; Rolón-Dow, 2005). In comparing the simultaneous but contradictory ways that Veronica and Vishon used the word *care* to describe both themselves and one another in Sections 1, 5, 7, 13, and 17, it becomes clear that, ironically, they spent more time talking about Veronica's "caring" than about Vishon's.

To provide some context, Veronica occasionally used this expression during class time, saying, for example, on days when assignments were due but few were turned in, "I don't want to hear excuses. I don't care," or, "If you have your work, thank you. If not, I don't care." On the surface, Veronica's multiple "I don't care" utterances seem to contradict social justice dispositions, like those described in Chapter 1 (refer to Figure 1.2); when a teacher says, "I don't care," she appears not to be practicing love, joy, hopefulness, or positivity. However, like Vishon, Veronica also can be understood as acting "hard" on some level through her use of the expression "I don't care."

As described earlier, Vishon keeps changing the subject when Veronica asks about his attitude, a seemingly evasive move; however, it is extremely important not to miss that he also is astutely inquiring into a contradiction he sensed in Veronica's discourse. Through his moves in this conversation, Vishon demonstrates how much he values and expects consistency in his teacher, and he calls attention to what he sees as an inconsistency. Vishon's decision to name and voice his confusion to his teacher—not just once but persistently (three times!)—actually suggests that many things were going right in this teacher/student interaction and in the relationship in which it occurred: He identifies both this staying-to-talk timespace and this teacher as worthy of his taking such significant risks.

Vishon's and Veronica's inquiries about each other's "caring" are held in tension for almost the entire conversation. The tension, and Vishon's confusion, is resolved only in Section 17, when Veronica finally makes her meaning explicit ("You're responsible for yourself. That's what I mean when I say I don't care. . . . I do care when I see a student who is bright and is just literally choosing to be lazy"). Prior to this, they performed two different notions of what "I don't care" means. The first meaning, which Vishon seems to understand Veronica to be saying, is "*I don't care about you, about whether you succeed.*" The second meaning, which Veronica seems to intend, is "*It doesn't matter; what you choose to do affects you, not me.*" What Veronica seems to have meant is that Vishon's choices would not affect her in any way; by bringing up Rashed as an example, she assures Vishon that she doesn't engage in coddling or hand-holding. This meaning is reminiscent of Melanie's comment to Antonio, discussed in Chapter 4, "It doesn't make *me* feel any way. It should make *you* feel *sad*!" However, Veronica's example is not enough to help Vishon understand or, possibly, believe her intent. It is not until Vishon says, "you don't care, so I don't care either" (Section 17) that it becomes clear how far Veronica's use of this simple expression may have backfired: Not only does it appear that Vishon has been misunderstanding it, but it also seems that this misunderstanding may have led him to act in ways that were actually the opposite of her intention.

Why might Vishon repeatedly have focused on how Veronica and other teachers know he's capable and on what Veronica means when she says she "doesn't care"? Aside from probing the disconnect he was experiencing between her words and her actions, might he also have been assuming that teachers should "care" only when a student's behavior was "affecting [others] in the class" (Section 13)? Testing her to see if she actually did care? Trying to prick her conscience and entice her to say explicitly that she actually *did* care? Whatever his motivation, it is difficult to imagine that his agentive, critical inquiry would have been possible in any other timespace. Further, it would have been difficult to predict that one of the most significant outcomes of his inquiry into Veronica's caring was a revelation about his own—about how his own "caring" was aligned with his understanding of Veronica's. Vishon's explanation, "That's . . . why I act like this, 'cause you say you don't care, so I don't care either" (Section 17), represents a departure from acting "hard," which was enabled by this timespace; it implies that, conversely, if Veronica *did* care, he would care as well. It is Vishon's persistent inquiry and finally his revelation that prompt Veronica both to state clearly what she means by "I don't care," and to use, for the first time, the words "I do care." As these moves demonstrate, even though this staying-to-talk conversation was initiated by Veronica, Vishon took it where *he* wanted it to go, a powerful demonstration of youth agency—a demonstration that can help increase ties to school.

CONCLUSION:
"REALIZE LOVE IN WORD AND DEED" BY STAYING TO TALK

No course in preservice teacher education programs typically focuses on preparing teachers to love their students, yet while loving youth is often what draws people to become teachers, it is also what teachers often feel they have the least opportunity to do. As bell hooks (2000) argues, because "all the great movements for social justice in our society have strongly emphasized a love ethic," and because there is a "mounting lovelessness in our culture," we need to work much harder "to know how to realize love in word and deed" (pp. xi, xxviii). This chapter argues that one important way for teachers to "realize love" is to engage in the practice of staying to talk with students with failing grades, students who also may be navigating pluralistic cultural identities. Veronica's interaction with Vishon represents the patterns that I witnessed among teachers who demonstrated their equity orientation and love for students by staying after class to talk to those who were struggling to pass. As this chapter describes, staying to talk is a powerful strategy in positioning both teachers and students toward retention. Given that all of the students I witnessed who engaged in staying to talk with their teachers went on to pass the class, I urge teachers to use this strategy intentionally and exuberantly with students they believe are falling through the cracks, particularly those with failing grades and those with whom they do not already have a personal connection. The after-class timespace represents an especially promising yet generally untapped resource for equity-oriented teachers. When teachers take full advantage of the "place for freedom" it represents, they, together with their students who are falling through the cracks, can realize love, the experience of which can create a sense of connection to one another and to the school community.

Below, I offer teachers several recommendations for overcoming two closely related, common obstacles—lacking boldness and lacking cultural knowledge—in order to begin regularly including staying-to-talk interactions as part of their teaching strategies, particularly with students who have failing grades.

Obstacle #1: Lacking Boldness or a Sense of Authority

This chapter recommends that teachers reach out to students who are failing through the cracks by asking them to stay to talk after class. But new teachers may be intimidated by the direct and somewhat uncomfortable nature of making such a request of a student. Many new high school teachers are only a few years older than the 9th and 10th graders they often are assigned to teach. In my study, the teachers were, on average, 8 years older than their students, young enough to be mistaken for students, a fact they often bemoaned. But as much as they may despise the "You look so young!" comments often directed at them, new teachers need not contribute to the mythology surrounding them by behaving in passive, unsure, or demure ways. New, equity-oriented teachers must overcome their resistance to initiate staying-to-talk meetings out of a desire to avoid conflict or out of fear of interfering with students' schedules or offending students. Students with failing grades will not be served by teachers' polite avoidance of the topic of their failure. Instead, like other pedagogical methods, staying-to-talk interactions become easier and more natural the more teachers practice them. To overcome the obstacle of lacking boldness or a sense of authority to initiate staying-to-talk meetings, I recommend the following:

- Mitigate staying-to-talk discomfort by framing your request to meet as a chance to ask students a question. For example, the request you make of a student during class could be as simple as, "Vishon, I have a question for you. Can we talk after class?" Then, when the classroom clears, you can ask a broad question to begin the meeting, such as, "How are you doing?" or one as pointed as, "I never get a chance to talk to you; how are you feeling about this class?" or, "I'm a little worried about your grade; can you tell me what I can do to help you succeed?"
- Consider, alternatively, inviting students to stay to talk by writing a note on work you're returning—homework, a paper they're writing, a quiz, or a test.
- Persistently remind the students of their unique strengths and gifts, helping them visualize how to use these assets toward academic success. If you aren't yet familiar with students' strengths and gifts, use staying-to-talk meetings to learn more about them and to be explicit about their promise in your class.

- Tell students that you care about their success and that you want them to succeed, and develop a plan of action together. Ask questions to find out what has been especially difficult for them and why, and, together, think through possible ways to overcome these difficulties. Acting with authority doesn't mean refraining from asking questions; often, it means quite the opposite. Nor does acting with authority mean telling students what to do; again, it often means quite the opposite.

Obstacle #2: Lacking Cultural Knowledge

When a student is failing a class despite the teacher's best efforts, it is natural for the teacher both to try to learn what factors are standing in the way of the student's success and to try to ameliorate those factors. But teachers may refrain from initiating a staying-to-talk meeting with students who are failing because they may be aware that they lack knowledge about the range of factors that may be at work in the students' lives. Although new teachers likely have taken required diversity coursework in their teacher preparation programs and therefore are likely to have been exposed to facts about various cultures, they may not yet have had opportunities to understand how these cultures can be at work in their classrooms. For example, while a new teacher might have learned that 41% of American children live in or near poverty and that this percentage is much higher, about 60%, for Black, Hispanic, and American Indian children (Koball & Jiang, 2018), the teacher might see a male student sleeping in class but not wonder whether he might be unable to stay awake because he worked the closing shift last night in order to help support his family. In such a situation, a new teacher might make the mistake of not talking with the student to find out what is causing his drowsiness, particularly if the teacher assumes that the student has put his head down as an act of protest, defiance, or boredom—possibilities that would be uncomfortable to broach and therefore easier to avoid confronting. Additionally, because new teachers harbor significant fears about their job security before earning tenure, they often are inclined to avoid any situation that might lead to conflict or attract attention. Thus, a new teacher's negotiation about whether to invite students to stay to talk also involves the navigation of the school's culture: Do colleagues typically engage in talking with students after class? How will such a move be viewed by colleagues, administrators, and parents? To overcome this obstacle as a new teacher, I recommend that you:

- Get to know all of your students as a matter of course so that you will have built a bridge both to extending such an invitation to talk and to talking with the student substantively. You can use a combination of strategies to get to know your students, from talking informally with them between classes, as discussed in Chapter 4, to having your students fill out get-to-know-you surveys with questions not only about their gifts, talents, and favorite things but also their needs as a learner. Of course, asking a student to stay to talk with you after class becomes much easier when it is not your first time really talking to him or her.

- Understand that cultural knowledge is important; however, cultural dispositions are also important. As Irizarry (2007) notes, "Culturally responsive pedagogy is about more than *what* teachers need to know about a specific group of students; it also involves *who they need to be* and *who they need to continuously become*" (p. 27, emphasis in original). You must earn students' respect through showing them respect, and it is through the dispositions of respecting and trusting your students, of being committed to learning continuously from and about them, of wanting the best for them, of being committed to helping them overcome barriers, that you will earn the respect of your students as well as of the broader community.

QUESTIONS FOR TEACHER REFLECTION, DISCUSSION, AND ACTION

1. How can use my time after class to talk with my students who currently have failing grades and to position them positively toward retention?

   a. Make a list of students who currently have failing grades. In what kinds of assignments have they been successful? Where are they struggling?

   b. What specific personal qualities indicate their potential?

   c. What patterns do I observe that are negatively affecting their grades in my class, and how can I help them make changes to these patterns?

   d. With which of the students' other teachers could I discuss possible strategies for working together to help the students succeed?

   e. What do I already know about them, inside and outside the classroom? In what specific ways do they perform their identities, such as topics they talk about, tattoos they have, or art or symbols they display on their backpacks?

   f. What would I like to know about them?

   g. How can I use the above information to construct questions and conversation starters?

   h. Do I have any students engaged in acting "hard"? Am I willing to meet with those who do, privately, after class, remembering to keep the classroom door open during all meetings?

i. On what specific date and between-class time can I commit to begin connecting with each student? On what second set of dates and times will I connect intentionally for a second time, perhaps engaging in dialogue about some of the above questions with them?

j. What can I do to sustain these relationships and to follow up on these initial interactions?

2. How can I structure my conversation with students who are failing in order to increase their agency? How and when can I allow them to determine the direction of our interactions?

3. Are my students' grades on private work (undertaken and submitted privately to me, like major assessments or individual projects) and their grades on public work (undertaken and submitted more publicly, such as seatwork or group projects) weighted equally, or is one weighted more heavily than the other? If they are of unequal weight, which students benefit? Is it mathematically possible for students who are acting "hard" to pass? If not, what changes can I make in order for them not to have to choose between earning the respect of their teachers and that of their peers?

CHAPTER 6

Conclusion

Interacting with a New Taxonomy for Equity-Oriented Teaching

During a high school class period I recently observed, a preservice teacher was giving students time to revise an essay. As they began the activity, I noticed that a student sitting near me wasn't sure where to find a key on-line resource. Since the preservice teacher was busy, I introduced myself to the student, asked for his name—Damian—and tried to help. When I couldn't find the resource either and saw that the host teacher was alone at his desk, I walked up to him and asked if he could show Damian and me how to find it. He came back with me, looked at Damian's screen displaying his work, and asked, "This is what you submitted? This is your essay?" Damian seemed taken aback by the questions, answering slowly in the affirmative. The teacher continued on, noting that the essay contained no paragraphs and that there should be paragraphs in an essay. Damian replied that of course he knew that but that when he copied his text from another application, it messed up his formatting. I nodded and empathized that the application he mentioned was "the worst!" for preserving formatting. He immediately turned to me with a simultaneous, "That's what's up," and fist bump before we all returned to locating the online resource.

Several aspects of this brief interaction sadden me. First, I am saddened that the host teacher demonstrated a deficit perspective in this interaction with Damian, with whom he had been working for months as his English teacher. He demonstrated this perspective both by seeming to assume that Damian did not know that essays should contain separate paragraphs and by reproaching him for submitting low-quality work. I am saddened that the host teacher made negative assessments of Damian and his work based on one quick glance at it. And although I was glad to have connected with Damian, I am saddened by his quick positive response to one small expression of empathy from someone who had been a stranger to him less than 5 minutes previously.

Most of all, I am saddened by the realization that countless inequitable interactions like this one are, like continuous ocean waves, eroding students' positive sense of themselves, of their school, and of their futures, not only in Damian's classroom but in classrooms everywhere. When directed at a student, teachers' comments such as, "This is what you submitted? This is your essay?" take on heightened importance when they occur, as they did here, between a White teacher and a student of color, and demonstrate how, along with the pushout microcultures discussed earlier, teacher/student interactions can be sites of racial microaggressions (Huber & Solórzano, 2015). Such harmful interactions, and the deficit perspectives that fuel them, have absolutely no place in our classrooms. Knowing that they persist alongside the kinds of equity-oriented interactions described in this book, however, lends a hopeful urgency to the work of ensuring that all teachers—new and experienced; elementary, secondary, and postsecondary; urban, suburban, and rural—know how to interact with their students, particularly their marginalized students, with the humane, radically compassionate, radically patient dispositions that characterize an equity orientation.

Having established in the previous chapters the importance of equity-oriented teacher/student interactions, in this conclusion I ask: What would happen if we truly prioritized them in teacher preparation programs? What if we de-prioritized everything else that might interfere with them? While the previous chapters discuss numerous recommendations for teachers, the remainder of this chapter is focused on implications for teacher educators. Namely, I propose a new taxonomy of knowledge domains for educational practice that positions "equity and social justice knowledge" and "context knowledge" as the foundational predecessors for all other categories. I emphasize how reorienting teacher preparation with this taxonomy can pave the way for teachers to prioritize their interactions with students and increase both student and teacher retention.

> What would happen if we truly prioritized equity-oriented teacher/student interactions in teacher preparation programs?
>
> What if we de-prioritized everything else that might interfere with them?

PRIORITIZING INTERACTIONS IN TEACHER PREPARATION

In her exit interview, Melanie reflected that during her first year as a teacher, developing relationships with students was an aspect of her professional practice that frequently "got lost." Although she returned the following year with a new approach, Melanie characterized her experience as a 1st-year teacher as "just trying to tread water"—a frightening but fairly common image among new teachers. Because so much of her time and energy was directed toward curriculum design and implementation, she wasn't able to be the relationship-focused teacher she wanted to be. Indeed, new teachers have so much on their plate, including adjusting to teaching in a new environment and getting to know the curriculum, that they tend to describe themselves as being in "survival mode," as another former student explained (Sam Young, personal communication, March 15, 2016). It is impossible for someone who is in an emergency situation and focused on their own survival, such as having to tread water, to help others. Teachers are no different.

Because teacher education historically has been structured to privilege teachers' content knowledge, pedagogical knowledge, pedagogical content knowledge, and curricular knowledge (Shulman, 1986, 1987) above student knowledge and equity knowledge, neither the deficit perspective of teachers like Damian's nor the survival mindset of new, equity-oriented teachers like Melanie and Sam should come as a surprise. Through required coursework, assignments, and fieldwork, teacher preparation programs can either undermine or increase their graduates' readiness to engage in equity-oriented interactions with their students even as 1st-year teachers, and I suggest that many of our teacher preparation programs are setting our equity-oriented teachers up for failure in this regard. Therefore, I urge teacher educators to critically examine their course of study to determine how well it is positioning graduates to create a pull-in culture in their classes that will position themselves and their students toward retention. As Sam went on to say, "Teaching for social justice is what helps you survive the first year. It invigorates you; developing relationships with students places discipline where it needs to be; and it makes you stay constantly connected to your purpose for teaching." Below, I offer recommendations for teacher preparation programs seeking to make reforms that will enable their graduates to emerge ready to engage in equity-oriented interactions.

Begin with Equity and Social Justice Knowledge

The modern teacher preparation programs modeled on the major knowledge domains identified by Shulman (1986, 1987) provide an important but insufficient framework and agenda for teachers' work with students. Despite Ladson-Billings's (1995b) call for reform, teacher preparation programs typically treat equity and social justice knowledge and context knowledge as 11th-hour additions to an undergraduate or graduate program of study, only if there is time, which, increasingly, with the intrusion of external performance assessments there is not. Such framing normalizes the status quo and neither provides the worldview nor creates the sense of urgency in teachers that minoritized students and their communities need and deserve.

As such, my first recommendation is for teacher educators to invert the traditional, Shulman-based knowledge domains and, instead, to prioritize the domains of equity and social justice knowledge and context knowledge, both chronologically and emphatically, making them not only the *first* focus but also the *foundation* for all subsequent focuses in the teacher preparation program (see Figure 6.1). In focusing on the first domain, equity and social justice knowledge, courses should privilege the voices of scholars, teachers, and students of color (refer to sources cited in Figure 1.2) and should emphasize specifically how inequities can be perpetuated in schools or can be interrupted through anti-racist, culturally sustaining methods of teaching. This focus also includes roles and dispositions for teachers that actively promote equity and justice in every aspect of their teaching practice. For example, teacher preparation programs can ensure not only that preservice teachers know the characteristics of a warm demander disposition (Ware, 2006) and can identify what it can look like in classroom but also that they practice being a warm demander in their fieldwork and that they receive feedback on their efforts. Other examples of equity-oriented teaching that teacher preparation programs can require preservice teachers to practice include viewing students with an asset perspective as opposed to a deficit perspective (Ladson-Billings, 1994) and engaging in racial literacies (Sealey-Ruiz & Greene, 2015) and equity literacies (Gorski, 2013). Teacher preparation programs should require that preservice teachers be able not only to define these paradigms but also to practice embodying them in their work with students during fieldwork and that they receive feedback on their efforts.

Figure 6.1. A New Taxonomy of Knowledge Domains for Equity-Oriented Teaching

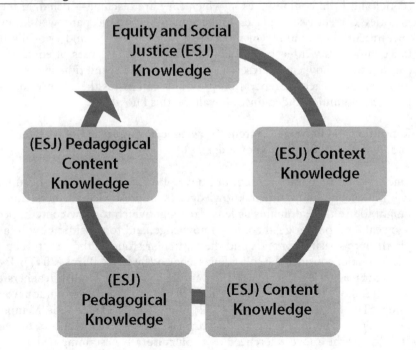

Privilege Context Knowledge

In this taxonomy, the second domain, context knowledge, is one that Shulman (1987) does include in his categories of teacher knowledge, but it is another area that teacher preparation programs frequently overlook. Yet when teacher education programs regard teaching as acontextual, they miss critical opportunities to prepare their graduates for success. Why? Geneva Gay (2000) addresses this issue extensively, noting that "many educators still believe that good teaching transcends place, people, time, and context. . . . Individuals who subscribe to this belief fail to realize that their standards of 'goodness' in teaching and learning are culturally determined and are not the same for all ethnic groups" (p. 22). Clearly, teachers cannot attune their practice with context unless they know their context well. Shulman (1987) defines educational context knowledge as "ranging from the workings of the group or classroom, the governance and financing of school districts, to the character of communities and cultures" (p. 8). Teacher educators should teach their preservice teachers to obtain and value this knowledge, view it through the lens of equity and social justice knowledge described above, and translate it into their actual preservice teaching practices so that they are ready to engage independently in these practices in their first teaching positions. Teacher preparation programs can create assignments and fieldwork through which preservice teachers are required to learn about the specific school and local communities in which they are teaching—including their histories; current issues, places, and events of importance; and well-known and treasured community members (e.g., Bieler, 2012)—and critically inquire into texts written by and about them using the lenses of equity and social justice knowledge. Preservice teachers should spend time in the communities, and teacher preparation programs can assess their knowledge of those communities to demonstrate valuing this knowledge.

Reposition and Reframe Content Knowledge, Pedagogical Knowledge, and Pedagogical Content Knowledge

Once teacher preparation programs have prioritized equity and social justice knowledge and context knowledge, their preservice teachers can be taught to use these domains as lenses through which to view content, pedagogical, and pedagogical content knowledge, and to consider how to apply them to specific contexts and the particular students they are teaching. For example, consider the following scenario (Bieler & Burns, 2017): Two different teacher educators ask their future secondary English teachers to write a 2-day lesson plan sequence for a 9th-grade short story unit on irony using "The Lesson" (Bambara, 1972) and "The Necklace" (de Maupassant, 1907). The first teacher educator asks her aspiring teachers to read and discuss the above-referenced texts on culturally sustaining pedagogies, racial literacy, and equity literacy before discussing lesson planning, while the second teacher educator focuses only on lesson-planning methods. Aspiring teachers taught by the first teacher educator would be more likely to notice and incorporate in their teaching how issues of poverty and race/ethnicity figure prominently in these two short stories, to consider how their knowledge of the school community could play a role in their framing of these stories, and to find ways to integrate their students' skills, interests, and inquiries as they distinguish among three types of irony. Aspiring teachers taught by the second teacher educator would likely only distinguish among three types of irony.

What would happen—to our teacher education programs, to our classrooms, and to the field of education—if it became the norm to expect preservice teachers to write lesson plans with an equity orientation from the very beginning? If graduates entered their first positions as teachers already knowing, for example, not just why *Romeo and Juliet* is a tragedy, how to teach drama, and how to help students navigate Shakespearean language, but also when and why modern versions of the play, such as *Romiette and Julio* (Draper, 2001), would be a good alternative; whether and how to teach a text in which suicide occurs, when the community recently has lost a member due to suicide; or how to talk about warring families when there is gang activity in the community? As Smagorinsky, Johnson, and Clayton (2014) argue, "The development of rich conceptions of issues surrounding educational diversity can never begin soon enough" (p. 133).

But why focus on teacher preparation programs' knowledge domains in a book arguing the importance of teacher/student interactions? My response is this: Only new teachers who are not overwhelmed, who are not merely "treading water" or "in survival mode," can prioritize interactions with students. And teacher preparation programs must help prevent their graduates from being overwhelmed and instead create conditions for their interactional success by fully preparing them as experts in all knowledge domains before they become full-time teachers. To provide this preparation effectively, teacher educators will need to carefully design the coursework to include active fieldwork in which preservice teachers interact directly with students rather than merely observe others' teaching. However, making this a positive experience requires a scaffolding of assignments that likely cannot fit into one or two methods courses taken during or immediately prior to student teaching.

> Only teachers who are not overwhelmed can prioritize interactions with students.

A CALL TO ACTION

Anyone who has spent time in classrooms can attest to the energy they contain. Emanating from the vitality and vibrancy of the youth within them, this energy can be witnessed in nearly constant talk. To those who love teaching, this constant talk is exciting and energizing on most days. It can feel like the rush of adrenaline that performers, like improvisational actors or musicians, feel when, having prepared their part, they take the stage. It can even feel like a reunion between friends.

Of all of the talk that animates our school buildings, the interactions between teachers and students are the heartbeat of schools. By listening carefully to this heartbeat, as I have argued here, we not only can discover a great deal about the general health of the classrooms and even the institutions in which they occur but also can estimate the lifespan of participants' connection to schools. But as important as it is to listen to our interactions diagnostically and to use these diagnoses toward rehabilitation, we also must ensure that these heartbeats are healthy, are strong, from the beginning and all throughout each student's and each teacher's life in schools. And as important as it is to diagnose heartbeats, we must ensure that we do not over-assess them; for just as the overuse of electrocardiograms and cardiac catheterizations can damage the very heartbeats they are designed to assess, overuse of teacher/student interaction assessments can cause stress on these heartbeats. Sometimes a world of meaning can be found in, a world of questions sparked by, a world of possibilities opened by even the briefest of interactions, even in the smallest spaces. They are worth our attention.

Epilogue

She's gonna dream up
The world she wants to live in
She's gonna dream out loud.

(U2, 1993, "Zooropa")

About 8 years after they opened their classrooms to me for the original study on which this book is based, Heather, Jasmine, Melanie, and Veronica took time to participate in a brief follow-up study. Although much had changed in their personal lives, all four teachers remained public high school English teachers. In this epilogue, I step aside, grateful for the opportunity to create space for these equity-oriented teachers, now experienced rather than new, to speak directly to you about whether and how their interactions with students and their commitments to equity-oriented classroom teaching have changed over the years and what their advice is for new and equity-oriented teachers. I have edited their words minimally and only to achieve cohesion or preserve anonymity.

1. **Are you still teaching in the same school in which you began your career? Why did you stay or leave?**

Veronica: Yes. I have continued there because there was an administrative change that allowed me to have a variety of opportunities. At one point, I was working diligently to find work at another school or outside of education. As luck would have it, there was a leadership change at the end of that summer. The school received a new principal, and, over time, and a new set of vice principals. This change opened the doors to various learning experiences that helped me further develop as a teacher and a leader.

Melanie: No. During my third year, the 9th- and 10th-grade teachers were offered an incentive having to do with student assessment. Because of this, our school went through a major transition, and I (along with five other teachers) was selected to be a part of the transition team. We showed great dedication to the school and commitment to student improvement, taking on extra leadership work in addition to our teaching positions. Ultimately, the teachers, with the support of the building administrator, requested compensation for this work but were denied by the superintendent.

After that meeting, I was disheartened, not to mention burnt out. There is a lot of pressure when you are a teacher who is responsible for student improvement on such an important assessment. I had worked tirelessly for my school both during the academic year and the summer, often sacrificing time from my personal life with no compensation. Although I loved my students, and their success brought me happiness, it is nice to be acknowledged for your hard work. Two months prior to that meeting, I was offered a position to work as an instructional coach in a turnaround district. Originally, I declined the position because I could not imagine leaving my school. But after that meeting and several other interactions with the superintendent, I was not sure that the district, at the time, was a place that I could continue growing as an educator. I held the instructional coach job for 2 years, and then I returned to teaching, where I'm in my fourth year.

Jasmine: Yes. This school is very diverse, allowing me to teach students from various ethnic groups, income levels, and cultural backgrounds. It is a great place to be teaching for social justice. There are many opportunities for teachable moments.

Heather: Yes. I like working there. I love the staff, and the students are generally decent. While I have *definitely* started to job search from time to time when it's a particularly "bad" year or the morale is very low, ultimately, I have a good deal. And now that I've been there for 12 years, moving to another district would likely mean less money and starting over (with material) from scratch. I'm just not in a position to do that, personally.

2. **What does "teaching for social justice" mean to you, and in what ways do you see yourself as a justice-oriented or equity-oriented teacher? And how, if at all, would you say that your beliefs about teaching for social justice and/or the ways that you practice your commitments to justice have changed since you began teaching?**

Melanie: Teaching for social justice means recognizing how privilege and power impact the classroom and its culture and teaching within that dynamic so that students don't feel oppressed or denied opportunities due to their race, gender, or other factors that could put them at a disadvantage.

I believe that now I am more aware of issues of injustice within the educational setting, and I am also more confident in pointing out those instances and speaking out against them.

Heather: While I'm not sure if this is exactly what it meant to me years ago, at this point, "teaching for social justice" means more about my attitude and response when my students appear "unjust" or biased in their commentary. It's become the way in which I try to treat each of my students equally, but that doesn't always mean everyone needs or requires "the same." I think, at the start of my career, I was more aggressive with my approach to exposing my students to a wide variety of perspectives from various sources/cultures. I'm sure a number of factors have contributed to the change—increased focus on prep for standardized assessments (being told to cover fewer units but "go deeper in [my] analysis," personal life changes, and so on).

    Veronica: Education is supposed to be "the great equalizer," but that is not true. Black and Brown kids are underserved, which has been true throughout history. For me, "teaching for social justice" means being skilled and ready to prepare *all* of the students who walk into my classroom. As I've gained more leadership opportunities over the years, I've tried to tackle the fundamental needs of students, as opposed to being concerned about assessment scores. Thinking forward is critical, so conversation often goes to college and career readiness. Ultimately, how can we teach and operate as an organization that gets as many doors open as possible for our students? Trying to keep options open for all students is where I feel that my work creates justice for students.

    I now better see and understand how the structure of education works. I won't say there are good and bad guys, but I will say that the various interests of leaders cause or lead to the cracks that students slip through. My commitment to social justice has not changed, but I better understand what I am up against. I did not fully understand this when I first started teaching, but I see and understand more now.

    Jasmine: Teaching for social justice means incorporating lessons that foster tolerance, using every selection of literature we read in class to discuss how discrimination affects society as a whole, and creating activities that require students to use different cultural lenses.

    I do not believe my beliefs about teaching for social justice have changed at all. I am still committed to teaching for change.

3. **How would you characterize your current style of interacting with your students? Is it different from how you interacted with them earlier in your career, and if so, how and why?**

    Heather: Friendly-but-not-friends, genuine, relaxed. The thought of what I seem like on those videos [from the original study] is a bit terrifying.

I imagine my responses are now very much shorter and businesslike to those questions I've heard millions of times from my students (the bathroom, missing work, grade panics, general whining about everyday tasks). While I like to think my personality is pretty similar, my patience is a little shorter than it used to be. I think that's actually a good thing.

Jasmine: My style of interaction is always professional, patient, and pleasant. I do not believe I am any different than I was 7 or 8 years ago. I am just as eager to help students through their struggles, and just as forgiving of their shortcomings. I believe I was already quite set in my mannerisms, and they extend beyond the classroom and my employment. It is simply my personal outlook: Treat others how you want to be treated.

Veronica: Positive and demanding come to mind first. On the day to day, I have a rapport with students that allows me to know them on a personal level. This allows me to craft assignments that are personally engaging. However, the interactions are also demanding because I receive a great deal of pushback from students and parents, there are varying expectations across classrooms, and it is tough to reach everyone in the room. I cannot claim perfection in my student interactions, but I put forth a great deal of effort for each student in my classroom.

Honestly, I've returned to some of my original practices. There were a few years where personal relationships took a back seat to meeting standards and getting through the curriculum. Simply put, it did not work. I was unhappy, and so were the students. About 2 years ago, I returned to my original practices. I try to show that I care personally. I talk to students one on one, I apologize if I make a mistake, I reach out to parents to make positive phone calls, etc. In the beginning, I tried to put myself out there for students; I wanted them to see me as a human. I returned to that practice, because it was best for me.

I maintain policies that hold me and students accountable: four bathroom passes per marking period, after-school help for those who need it, applause when warranted, public acknowledgment of student growth, one-on-one conversations in the face of challenges. These are just a few things that help to create a positive learning community for myself and students.

Melanie: The way I interact with my students is professional yet fun-loving and "real." I know this may sound cliché, but I treat the students as I would want my own child to be treated. I do not yell at students or disrespect or embarrass them in front of their peers. I am nurturing yet firm.

I try to be their biggest cheerleader when they need encouragement, and I acknowledge their effort when they are making improvements. In addition, my students know that I "do not play" when it comes to their academics. I have high standards for all students who enter my class, but I also meet them where they are, given the different skill sets that each student brings. I am direct and will let them know if they need to step it up.

There are definitely aspects of my interactions with students that have changed. I know that I have grown more patient, which I find interesting because many teachers have told me that the opposite has happened to them.

I joke around more with my students, and I am more comfortable at letting them see my mistakes. During the first couple years of teaching, I felt like I had to have everything together and that I couldn't make a mistake. I am much more relaxed in that aspect.

I also respond to student misbehavior differently than I did in the beginning of my career. In the beginning of my career, I internalized the majority of the things that happened in class. For example, if a student put her head down, it was because I was boring and a terrible teacher. Now I understand that it isn't always about me and my lesson. There are other factors that can contribute to how that student is feeling.

4. **Were you surprised by the findings that the focal students who went on to fail English initiated academic-focused interactions with their English teachers at a higher rate than all of the other students and that they initiated social interactions with them at the lowest rate of all students?**

Jasmine: It actually does make sense that students who do not have a strong connection to the teacher do not perform as well as the students who do. I have noticed, as well, that students who do not speak to me about their home life, their friendships, and their personal struggles also report for extra help less than the students who have more social interactions with me. These students appear to hold more in emotionally, have less people with whom they are comfortable expressing their feelings, and are likely to have personal battles that impede their learning and make it difficult to focus on their education. Many of the students who have failed my class have had struggles that would cause many adults to lose focus of their goals. A few students have spoken to me after their personal struggles decreased; they wanted me to know they were just dealing with too much and that I did not do anything wrong. It is always heartbreaking to discover what they were silently dealing with that prevented them from focusing in class and that kept from wanting to share with the staff at school. Just the end of last school year, a student who was particularly quiet stopped coming to school right before finals. I later discovered she was admitted to a mental health facility. I could tell prior to her absences that something was troubling her, but she always kept her discussions about the assignments, even when I would directly ask her if she needed to talk about anything not related to her academics. The look in her eyes told me there was something eating at her, but she never spoke about it. I always worry about my students who do not engage in social interactions, and this research has confirmed that my worry is warranted.

Melanie: Yes, I am a little surprised at these findings. I think as educators, we would naturally assume that students who fail are often off task during class time, so it is interesting to see that this is not always the case.

These findings reminded me of a TED Talk I watched about 4 years ago—Rita Pierson's "Every Kid Needs a Champion" (2013). In the video, Pierson discusses the idea that relationships are the foundation of education. She makes the point that kids won't learn from someone that they don't like or have a good relationship with. So while the student(s) could have been asking more academic questions, maybe the relationship between the teacher and student wasn't there, which impacted that student's academic achievement.

I know that in my career, there were times when I was not always the best at breaking down those barriers between myself and at-risk students, and I have often wondered how I could have better helped them.

Heather: Wow. I'm surprised at the student-initiated academic interactions, but not so much as the lower rate of social interactions. That said, I'm wondering if I could have initiated more social interactions with those students and made some difference? Then I think about the hundred students I see during the day and the pressure to teach course material, let's be real, to the test, and . . . how many more of those social interactions can I fit in? I know there's more to a course failure than the number of times I speak with a student about his/her life, but that information makes me want to start focusing again on the "kids," more than the "students," if you know what I mean.

Veronica: Humans perform better when they feel valued and personally connected. The social aspect of education is critical. I've worked with students who are developmentally challenged, autistic, and those who have "Swiss cheese" literacy skills and those who are above and beyond grade level. Regardless of their levels, I get the best work out of students who know that I care about them in and out of school.

One girl in particular comes to mind. She was an occasional distraction in class, but never malicious. She wanted to go to honors ELA because general ELA was boring. She explicitly wanted more challenging work; however, when I reviewed her academic history and started collecting her work submissions, I noted some glaring issues in her comprehension and writing skills. Not only did I convince her to stay after school for additional support, but I also started buying a variety of literary and informational texts for her to read. She needed exposure and practice. By the end of that school year, she tested into honors ELA without a problem. She and I literally jumped up and down in the hallway together. She went on to be a student leader and received multiple scholarships for college. In years past, she was pushed along. Our personal connection, which took time and effort, helped her attain her end goal.

Students do not want to fail. They need a reason to succeed.

5. **What, in your experience, are the biggest reasons why students end up failing English for the year, and how do you think English teachers can prevent these failures?**

Veronica: One reason is curriculum that is so jam-packed that there is no place for remediation. Districts claim to want data-based instruction but then leave no wiggle room for students and teachers. Students should receive depth as opposed to trying to learn so much during the course of a semester [half a school year].

Second, parents can be a problem. Those who are absent fail to support the student and teacher. Those who are overbearing undermine the teacher's intentions. This is *not* a generalization that all parents are "bad," but some definitely add to the challenge of helping a student.

Third, any district that does not listen to the feedback and ideas of the instructors is doomed to fail or spin its wheels.

Melanie: These are not listed in any particular order, but several reasons why students fail are a lack of preparation, outside resources or support, self-advocacy, or motivation. The structure of the school/district can also play a role.

Although trying to motivate someone is difficult and oftentimes impossible given that you cannot force anyone to act a certain way, I think that many of the above reasons can be influenced by the teacher and school community.

Heather: It's oversimplifying it, but I think it's a combination of a student's connection to the material, respect for the teacher, placement in a course that matches their skill level, and the attitude toward school and work that's been cultivated in their home. A teacher can attempt to influence part of that list, but there are definitely influences outside of school that have shaped a student long before 9th or 10th grade; those factors are often beyond a teacher's reach.

Jasmine: In my department, the summative essays and unit assessments are the biggest reasons for failures. Summative assessments make up 70% of students' marking period grades; both the unit assessments and the essays are summative. The teachers are required to have only three summative assessments per marking period. This is a problem because the marking period grades are based on three heavily weighted scores; if any of the scores are failing grades, or worse, a zero, the student may not be able to recover. Also, many students are not completing the essays at home. A few years ago, there was a big administrative push to stop using class time to type essays. The expectation was that students should use their time and resources at home to complete the essays. This is not what was happening. I have since switched to in-class essays as a default. The students only have 1 day to type; however, they are required to complete a detailed outline of the topic prior to the day they type. This has drastically decreased the amount of zeroes on essays.

I have also begun creating more assessments than required and making the added assessments creative projects instead of another multiple-choice or short answer assessment. It is also my policy to have the students make up any missed assessment in class the very day they return to school. I see less failed summative scores with these methods. If the entire ELA department used my methods for ensuring the work is completed, I believe we would have fewer failures.

6. **Finally, what is your advice for new, equity-oriented teachers about interacting with students—either students in general or, specifically, students who have a failing or close-to-failing grade?**

Melanie: The first piece of advice that I would give is, don't assume that you know what is going on with the student or that the student is just lazy. Get other people involved, such as the family, other teachers, and the counselor. Also, make sure that you are doing everything within your scope to help the student. That means keeping in contact with the family, offering one-on-one help, and having honest conversations about the class, your expectations, and the student's level of work.

Heather: Any kind of appropriate personal connection can be helpful; even if a student fails the course, your influence may continue beyond the report card.

Jasmine: My advice to new teachers is to be flexible, have patience, inquire about students' home lives early, make connections with the students and parents as much as possible, and do not take their attitudes, silence, or other unfavorable behavior personally. Keep in mind that life is throwing lemons at them as well. Know that your impact is felt, even if you do not see it. Trust yourself to be effective, and never stop learning. As far as the content of your lessons, you may not have a say in what you teach, but you can always use the material to discuss social justice, either by focusing on the obvious social justice or injustice, or by pointing out what points of view are not included in the text. In English classes, make the students question the motivations of the authors, the characters, and even, at times, the motives for selecting a particular text. The more they question, the more they understand.

Veronica: Find out *why*! Don't assume the student just won't or just can't. There is always a reason why. When possible, figure it out and use it to your benefit. Does the student have a history of failing? Does she or he have an unstable living situation? Is the student apathetic about education in general? Are expectations at home low? Also, don't forget that the student is just as human as you. Even when it is difficult to do so, try to approach the situation with grace.

References

Achinstein, B., Ogawa, R. T., Sexton, D., & Freitas, C. (2010). Retaining teachers of color: A pressing problem and a potential strategy for "hard-to-staff" schools. *Review of Educational Research, 80*(1), 71–107.

Ahlquist, R., Gorski, P., & Montaño, T. (2011). *Assault on kids: How hyperaccountability, corporatization, deficit ideologies, and Ruby Payne are destroying our schools.* New York, NY: Peter Lang.

Allensworth, E. M., & Easton, J. Q. (2007, July). *What matters for staying on-track and graduating in Chicago public high schools: A close look at course grades, failures, and attendance in the freshman year.* Chicago, IL: Consortium on Chicago School Research.

Alliance for Excellent Education. (2011, November). *The high cost of high school dropouts: What the nation pays for inadequate high schools.* Retrieved from all4ed.org/reports-factsheets/the-high-cost-of-high-school-dropouts-what-the-nation-pays-for-inadequate-high-schools/

Anyon, J. (1980). Social class and the hidden curriculum of work. *Journal of Education, 162*(1), 67–92.

Ayers, W. (2004). *Teaching the personal and political: Essays on hope and justice.* New York, NY: Teachers College Press.

Baker-Bell, A., Butler, T., & Johnson, L. (2017). The pain and the wounds: A call for Critical Race English Education in the wake of racial violence. *English Education, 49*(2), 116–128.

Balfanz, R., Bridgeland, J. M., Fox, J. H., DePaoli, J. L., Ingram, E. S., & Maushard, M. (2014). *Building a Grad Nation: Progress and challenge in ending the high school dropout epidemic.* Baltimore, MD: Everyone Graduates Center. Retrieved from www.americaspromise.org/building-grad-nation-report

Balfanz, R., & Letgers, N. (2004). *Locating the dropout crisis: Which high schools produce the nation's dropouts? Where are they located? Who attends them?* (Report 70). Baltimore, MD: Center for Research on the Education of Students Placed At Risk. Retrieved from new.every1graduates.org/wp-content/uploads/2012/03/Locating_the_Dropout_Crisis.pdf

Bambara, T. C. (1972). The lesson. Retrieved from iupui.edu/~l105onln/docs/The_Lesson.pdf

Bandura, A. (2001). Social cognitive theory: An agentic perspective. *Annual Review of Psychology, 52*, 1–26.

Banks, J. A. (2004). Multicultural education: Characteristics and goals. In J. A. Banks & C. M. Banks (Eds.), *Multicultural education: Issues and perspectives* (7th ed., pp. 3–32). Hoboken, NJ: Wiley.

Banks, J. A. (2007). Series foreword. In C. D. Lee (Ed.), *Culture, literacy, and learning: Taking bloom in the midst of the whirlwind* (pp. xi–xv). New York, NY: Teachers College Press.

Bell, L. A. (2007). Theoretical foundations for social justice education. In M. Adams, L. A. Bell, & P. Griffin (Eds.), *Teaching for diversity and social justice* (2nd ed., pp. 1–14). New York, NY: Routledge.

Benitez, M. (2010). Resituating culture centers within a social justice framework: Is there room for examining Whiteness? In L. Patton (Ed.), *Culture centers in higher education: Perspectives on identity, theory, and practice* (pp. 119–136). Sterling, VA: Stylus.

Berger, J. (1984). *Ways of seeing.* New York, NY: Viking.

Bhabha, H. K. (1994). *The location of culture.* New York, NY: Routledge.

Bieler, D. (2004). *"Inventing what we desire": Reconceptualizing "mentoring" relationships with student-teachers as dialogic praxis* (Unpublished doctoral dissertation). University of Pennsylvania, Philadelphia, PA.

Bieler, D. (2010). Dialogic praxis in teacher preparation: A discourse analysis of mentoring talk. *English Education, 42*(4), 391–426.

Bieler, D. (2011). Lessons from NETS: New English Teachers for Social Justice. *English Leadership Quarterly, 33*(4), 4–9.

Bieler, D. (2012). Possibilities for achieving social justice ends through standardized means. *Teacher Education Quarterly, 39*(3), 85–102.

Bieler, D. (2013). Strengthening new teacher agency through holistic mentoring. *English Journal, 102*(3), 23–32.

Bieler, D., & Burns, L. (2017). The critical centrality of social justice in English education. In H. Hallman (Ed.), *Innovations in pre-service English language arts teacher education* (pp. 147–163). Castle Hill, Australia: Emerald Press.

Bieler, D., Holmes, S., & Wolfe, E. (2017). Patterns in the initial teaching assignments of secondary English teachers: Implications for teacher agency and retention. *The New Educator, 13*(1), 22–40.

Bieler, D., & Young, S. (Forthcoming). A look into leaving: Learning from one equity-oriented teacher's resignation. In B. Charest & K. Sjostrom (Eds.), *Unsettling education: Searching for ethical footing in a time of reform.* New York, NY: Peter Lang.

Borman, G. D., & Dowling, N. M. (2008). Teacher attrition and retention: A meta-analytic and narrative review of the research. *Review of Educational Research, 78*(3), 369–409.

Bowers, A. J., Sprott, R., & Taff, S. A. (2013). Do we know who will drop out? A review of the predictors of dropping out of high school: Precision, sensitivity, and specificity. *The High School Journal, 96*(2), 77–100.

Boyd, D., Grossman, P., Ing, M., Lankford, H., Loeb, S., & Wyckoff, J. (2011).

The influence of school administrators on teacher retention decisions. *American Educational Research Journal, 48*(2), 303–333.

Brandt, D., & Clinton, K. (2002). Limits of the local: Expanding perspectives on literacy as a social practice. *Journal of Literacy Research, 34*(3), 337–356.

Burris, J., & Roberts, R. D. (2012, February). Dropping out of high school: Prevalence, risk factors, and remediation strategies. *ETS R&D Connections, 18.*

Cassidy, W., & Bates, A. (2005). "Drop-outs" and "push-outs": Finding hope at a school that actualizes the ethic of care. *American Journal of Education, 112*(1), 66–102.

Christensen, L. (2009). *Teaching for joy and justice: Re-imagining the language arts classroom.* Milwaukee, WI: Rethinking Schools.

Christensen, L. (2010). *NWP in person: Linda Christensen.* Retrieved from www.youtube.com/watch?v=FVV4JZNohhQ

Cochran-Smith, M. (2004). *Walking the road: Race, diversity, and social justice in teacher education.* New York, NY: Teachers College Press.

Collins, P. H. (1998). *Fighting words: Black women and the search for justice.* Minneapolis, MN: University of Minnesota Press.

Collins, P. H. (2000). *Black feminist thought: Knowledge, consciousness, and the politics of empowerment* (2nd ed.). New York, NY: Routledge.

Compton-Lilly, C., & Halverson, E. (Eds.). (2014). *Space and time in literacy research.* New York, NY: Routledge.

Dance, L. J. (2001). Shadows, mentors, and surrogate fathers: Effective schooling as critical pedagogy for inner-city boys. *Sociological Focus, 34*(4), 399–415.

Darling-Hammond, L., French, J., & Garcia-Lopez, S. (2002). *Learning to teach for social justice.* New York, NY: Teachers College Press.

de Maupassant, G. (1907). The necklace. In B. Matthews (Ed.), *The short-story: Specimens illustrating its development.* New York, NY: American Book Company. Retrieved from www.bartleby.com/195/1020.html

Delpit, L. (2006). Language diversity and learning. In E. Lee, D. Menkart, & M. Okazawa-Rey (Eds.), *Beyond heroes and holidays: A practical guide to K–12 anti-racist, multicultural education and staff development* (pp. 154–164). Washington, DC: Teaching for Change.

DeStigter, T. (2008). Lifting the veil of ignorance: Thoughts on the future of social justice teaching. In sj Miller, L.B. Beliveau, T. DeStigter, D. Kirkland, & P. Rice (Eds.), *Narratives of social justice teaching: How English teachers negotiate theory and practice between preservice and inservice spaces* (pp. 121–144). New York, NY: Peter Lang.

DeStigter, T. (2015). On the ascendance of argument: A critique of the assumptions of academe's dominant form. *Research in the Teaching of English, 50*(1), 11–34.

Dignity in Schools. (2011). National resolution for ending school pushout. Retrieved from www.dignityinschools.org/files/DSC_National_Resolution.pdf

Dobo, N. (2014, March 18). Speakers call for a new mindset in media, schools, public life. *The News Journal*. Retrieved from www.delawareonline.com/story/news/local/2014/03/18/speakers-call-for-a-new-mindset-in-media-schools-public-life/6590597/

Dover, A. G. (2013). Teaching for social justice: From conceptual frameworks to classroom practices. *Multicultural Perspectives, 15*(1), 3–11.

Draper, S. (2001). *Romiette and Julio*. New York, NY: Atheneum Books.

Duncan, G. A. (2000). Urban pedagogies and the celling of adolescents of color. *Social Justice, 27*(3), 29–42.

Duncan-Andrade, J. (2007). Gangstas, wankstas, and ridas: Defining, developing, and supporting effective teachers in urban schools. *International Journal of Qualitative Studies in Education, 20*(6), 617–638.

Dyson, A. H., & Genishi, C. (2005). *On the case: Approaches to language and literacy research*. New York, NY: Teachers College Press.

Eggins, S., & Slade, D. (1997). *Analyzing casual conversation*. Herndon, VA: Cassell.

Emdin, C. (2016). *For White folks who teach in the hood . . . and the rest of y'all too: Reality pedagogy and urban education*. Boston, MA: Beacon Press.

Fecho, B. (2004). *"Is this English?" Race, language, and culture in the classroom*. New York, NY: Teachers College Press.

Feldman, D. L., Smith, A. T., & Waxman, B. L. (2017). *Why we drop out: Understanding and disrupting student pathways to leaving school*. New York, NY: Teachers College Press.

Fine, M. (1991). *Framing dropouts*. Albany, NY: State University of New York Press.

Finn, J. (1989). Withdrawing from school. *Review of Educational Research, 59*, 117–142.

Fisher, M. T. (2007). *Writing in rhythm: Spoken word poetry in urban classrooms*. New York, NY: Teachers College Press.

Flett, M. R., Gould, D., Griffes, K. R., & Lauer, L. (2013). Tough love for underserved youth: A comparison of more and less effective coaching. *The Sport Psychologist, 27*(4), 325–337.

Foster, M. (1997). *Black teachers on teaching*. New York, NY: New Press.

Freedman, S. W., & Appleman, D. (2009). "In it for the long haul"—How teacher education can contribute to teacher retention in high-poverty, urban schools. *Journal of Teacher Education, 60*(3), 323–337.

Freire, P. (2000). *Pedagogy of the oppressed* (30th anniversary ed.). New York, NY: Continuum. (Original work published 1970)

Fujiyoshi, K. F. (2015). Becoming a social justice educator: Emerging from the pits of Whiteness into the light of love. *Democracy & Education, 23*(1), 1–6.

Gay, G. (2000). *Culturally responsive teaching: Theory, research, and practice*. New York, NY: Teachers College Press.

Gay, G. (2002). Preparing for culturally responsive teaching. *Journal of Teacher Education, 53*(2), 106–116.

Gee, J. (1996). *Social linguistics and literacies: Ideology in discourses* (2nd ed.). New York, NY: Routledge Falmer.

Gee, J. P. (2014). *An introduction to discourse analysis: Theory and method* (4th ed.). New York, NY: Routledge.

Gilbert, A., & Yerrick, R. (2001). Same school, separate worlds: A sociocultural study of identity, resistance, and negotiation in a rural, lower track science classroom. *Journal of Research in Science Teaching, 38*(5), 574–598.

Gorski, P. C. (2013). *Reaching and teaching students in poverty: Strategies for erasing the opportunity gap.* New York, NY: Teachers College Press.

Greene, M. (1988). *The dialectic of freedom.* New York, NY: Teachers College Press.

Greene, M. (1993). Diversity and inclusion: Toward a curriculum for human beings. *Teachers College Record, 95*(2), 211–221.

Greene, M. (1995). *Releasing the imagination: Essays on education, the arts, and social change.* San Francisco, CA: Jossey-Bass.

Greene, M. (1998). Introduction: Teaching for social justice. In W. Ayers, J. A. Hunt, & T. Quinn (Eds.), *Teaching for social justice* (pp. xxvii–xlvi). New York, NY: New Press & Teachers College Press.

Gutierréz, K., Rymes, B., & Larson, J. (1995). Script, counterscript, and underlife in the classroom: James Brown versus *Brown v. Board of Education. Harvard Educational Review, 65*(3), 445–471.

Haddix, M., & Price-Dennis, D. (2013). Urban fiction and multicultural literature as transformative tools for preparing English teachers for diverse classrooms. *English Education, 45*(3), 247–283.

Haddix, M. M., & Rojas, M. A. (2011). (Re)Framing teaching in urban classrooms: A poststructural (re)reading of critical literacy as curricular and pedagogical practice. In V. Kinloch (Ed.), *Urban literacies: Critical perspectives on language, learning, and community* (pp. 111–124). New York, NY: Teachers College Press.

Hall, S., Evans, J., & Nixon, S. (Eds.). (1997). *Representation: Cultural representations and signifying practices.* London, UK: Sage.

Harris, W. (2010, March 31). Dropped out? No, pushed out. Retrieved from thenotebook.org/articles/2010/03/31/dropped-out-no-pushed-out

Heckman, J. J., & Lafontaine, P. A. (2010). The American high school graduation rate: Trends and levels. *Review of Economics and Statistics, 92*, 244–262.

Hill, M. L. (2016). *Nobody: Casualties of America's war on the vulnerable, from Ferguson to Flint and beyond.* New York, NY: Atria Books.

Hoffman, L. (2007). Numbers and types of public elementary and secondary education agencies from the Common Core of Data: School year 2005–06 (NCES 2007-353). U.S. Department of Education. Washington, DC: National Center for Education Statistics, U.S. Department of Education. Retrieved from nces.ed.gov/pubs2007/2007353.pdf

Holland, D., Lachicotte, W., Skinner, D., & Cain, C. (1998). *Identity and agency in cultural worlds.* Cambridge, MA: Harvard University Press.

hooks, b. (1994). *Te∗ching to transgress: Education as the practice of freedom.* New York, NY: Routledge.

hooks, b. (2000). *All about love: New visions.* New York, NY: HarperCollins.

Huber, L. P., & Solórzano, D. G. (2015). Racial microaggressions as a tool for critical race research. *Race Ethnicity and Education, 18*(3), 297–320.

Hull, G., & Schultz, K. (Eds.). (2001). *School's out: Bridging out-of-school literacies with classroom practice.* New York, NY: Teachers College Press.

Ingersoll, R. M. (2002). The teacher shortage: A case of wrong diagnosis and wrong prescription. *NASSP Bulletin, 86*(631), 16–31.

Ingersoll, R. M. (2003). *Is there really a teacher shortage?* Philadelphia: Consortium for Policy Research in Education, University of Pennsylvania.

Ingersoll, R. M. (2007). Short on power, long on responsibility. *Educational Leadership, 65*(1), 20–25.

Ingersoll, R. M., & Connor, R. (2009, April). *What the national data tell us about minority and Black teacher turnover.* Paper presented at the annual meeting of the American Educational Research Association, San Diego, CA.

Ingersoll, R. M., & May, H. (2011). *Recruitment, retention and the minority teacher shortage* (Consortium for Policy Research in Education Research Report #RR-69). Retrieved from repository.upenn.edu/gse_pubs/226

Ingersoll, R. M., & Strong, M. (2011). The impact of induction and mentoring for beginning teachers: A critical review of the research. *Review of Educational Research, 81*(2), 201–233.

Irizarry, J. (2007). Ethnic and urban intersections in the classroom: Latino students, hybrid identities, and culturally responsive pedagogy. *Multicultural Perspectives, 9*(3), 21–28.

Jocson, K. M. (2006). "There's a better word": Urban youth rewriting their social worlds through poetry. *Journal of Adolescent and Adult Literacy, 49*(8), 700–707.

Jordan, J. (2002). *Some of us did not die: New and selected essays of June Jordan.* New York, NY: Basic/Civitas Books.

Juday, L. J. (2015). *The changing shape of America's cities.* Charlottesville, VA: Weldon Cooper Center Demographics Research Group, University of Virginia. Available at demographics.coopercenter.org/the-changing-shape-of-american-cities

Kirkland, D. E. (2013). *A search past silence: The literacy of young Black men.* New York, NY: Teachers College Press.

Koball, H., & Jiang, Y. (2018, January). *Basic facts about low-income children: Children under 18 years, 2016.* New York, NY: National Center for Children in Poverty, Mailman School of Public Health, Columbia University. Retrieved from www.nccp.org/publications/pdf/text_1194.pdf

Kozol, J. (1991). *Savage inequalities: Children in America's schools.* New York, NY: Random House.

Kumashiro, K. (2004). *Against common sense: Teaching and learning toward social justice.* New York, NY: RoutledgeFalmer.

Ladson-Billings, G. (1994). *The dreamkeepers: Successful teachers of African American children*. San Francisco, CA: Jossey-Bass.

Ladson-Billings, G. (1995a). But that's just good teaching! The case for culturally relevant pedagogy. *Theory into Practice, 34*(3), 159–165.

Ladson-Billings, G. (1995b). Toward a theory of culturally relevant pedagogy. *American Educational Research Journal, 32*(3), 465–491.

Ladson-Billings, G. (1997). I know why this doesn't feel empowering: A critical race analysis of critical pedagogy. In P. Freire, J. W. Fraser, D. Macedo, T. McKinnon, & W. T. Stokes (Eds.), *Mentoring the mentor: A critical dialogue with Paulo Freire* (pp. 127–141). New York, NY: Peter Lang.

Ladson-Billings, G. (2005). *Beyond the big house: African American educators on teacher education*. New York, NY: Teachers College Press.

Lave, J., & Wenger, E. (1991). *Situated learning: Legitimate peripheral participation*. Cambridge, UK: Cambridge University Press.

Lawrence-Lightfoot, S. (1983). *The good high school: Portraits of character and culture*. New York, NY: Basic Books.

Leander, K. M., & Sheehy, M. (Eds.). (2004). *Spatializing literacy research and practice*. New York, NY: Peter Lang.

Lee, C. D. (2007). *Culture, literacy, and learning: Taking bloom in the midst of the whirlwind*. New York, NY: Teachers College Press.

Lee, V. E., & Burkham, D. T. (2003). Dropping out of high school: The role of school organization and structure. *American Educational Research Journal, 40*(2), 353–393.

Lewis, C., Enciso, P., & Moje, E. B. (2007). *Reframing sociocultural research on literacy: Identity, agency, and power*. Mahwah, NJ: Erlbaum.

Lortie, D. (1975). *Schoolteacher: A sociological study*. Chicago, IL: University of Chicago Press.

Massey, D. (1994). *Space, place, and gender*. Minneapolis, MN: University of Minnesota Press.

Maybin, J. (2007). Literacy under and over the desk: Oppositions and heterogeneity. *Language and Education, 21*(6), 515–530.

McCann, T. M., Johannessen, L. R., & Ricca, B. P. (2005). *Supporting beginning English teachers: Research and implications for teacher education*. Urbana, IL: National Council of Teachers of English.

McVee, M .B., Brock, C. H., & Glazier, J. A. (2011). *Sociocultural positioning in literacy: Exploring culture, discourse, narrative, and power in diverse educational contexts*. Cresskill, NJ: Hampton Press.

Mitchell, T. D. (2008). Traditional vs. critical service-learning: Engaging the literature to differentiate two models. *Michigan Journal of Community Service Learning, 14*(2), 50–65.

Moje, E. B., McIntosh, K. C., Kramer, K., Ellis, L., Carrillo, R., & Collazo, T. (2004). Working toward third space in content area literacy: An examination of everyday funds of knowledge and discourse. *Reading Research Quarterly, 39*(1), 38–70.

Moll, L. C., Amanti, C., Neff, D., & Gonzalez, N. (1992). Funds of knowledge for teaching: Using a qualitative approach to connect homes and classrooms. *Theory into Practice, 31*(2), 132–141.

Morrell, E., & Duncan-Andrade, J. (2005). Popular culture and critical media pedagogy in secondary literacy classrooms. *International Journal of Learning, 12*, 1–11.

Morris, M. W. (2016). *Pushout: The criminalization of Black girls in school.* New York, NY: New Press.

Murray, J. (1997). "Agency," *Hamlet* on the Holodeck. In R. Packer & K. Jordan (Eds.), *Multimedia: From Wagner to virtual reality* (p. 381). New York, NY: Norton.

Neild, R. C., Stoner-Eby, S., & Furstenberg, F. F. (2001). *Connecting entrance and departure: The transition to ninth grade and high school dropout.* Retrieved from eric.ed.gov/?id=EJ798244

Nieto, S. (1999). *The light in their eyes: Creating multicultural learning communities.* New York, NY: Teachers College Press.

Nieto, S. (2003). *What keeps teachers going?* New York, NY: Teachers College Press.

Normore, A. H. (2008). *Leadership for social justice: Promoting equity and excellence through inquiry and reflective practice.* Charlotte, NC: Information Age.

Oakes, J. (1985). *Keeping track: How schools structure inequality.* New Haven, CT: Yale University Press.

Osterman, K. F. (2000). Students' need for belonging in the school community. *Review of Educational Research, 70*(3), 323–367.

Paris, D. (2012). Culturally sustaining pedagogy: A needed change in stance, terminology, and practice. *Educational Researcher, 41*(3), 93–97.

Paris, D., & Alim, H. S. (2014). What are we seeking to sustain through culturally sustaining pedagogy? A loving critique forward. *Harvard Educational Review, 84*(1), 85–100.

Paris, D., & Alim, H. S. (Editors). (2017). *Culturally sustaining pedagogies: Teaching and learning for justice in a changing world.* New York, NY: Teachers College Press.

Paris, D., & Winn, M. T. (2014). *Humanizing research: Decolonizing qualitative inquiry with youth and communities.* Thousand Oaks, CA: Sage.

Peterson, B. (1999). Foreword—My journey as a critical teacher: Creating schools as laboratories for social justice. In I. Shor & C. Pari (Eds.), *Education is politics: A tribute to the life and work of Paulo Freire* (pp. xi–xxii). Portsmouth, NH: Boynton/Cook.

Picower, B. (2012). *Practice what you teach: Social justice education in the classroom and the streets.* New York, NY: Routledge.

Pierson, R. (2013). Every kid needs a champion. Retrieved from www.ted.com/talks/rita_pierson_every_kid_needs_a_champion

Renn, A. M. (2014, September 14). The new donut. Retrieved from www.urbanophile.com/2014/09/14/the-new-donut/

Rios, V. M. (2006). The hyper-criminalization of Black and Latino male youth in the era of mass incarceration. *Souls, 8*(2), 40–54.

Ris, E. (2016, May 10). The problem with teaching "grit" to poor kids? They already have it. Here's what they really need. *Washington Post.* Retrieved from www.washingtonpost.com/news/answer-sheet/wp/2016/05/10/the-problem-with-teaching-grit-to-poor-kids-they-already-have-it-heres-what-they-really-need/?utm_term=.0ce5307a6e4e

Rockquemore, K. A. (2014, February 10). When it comes to mentoring, the more the merrier. *Vitae.* Retrieved from chroniclevitae.com/news/326-when-it-comes-to-mentoring-the-more-the-merrier

Rolón-Dow, R. (2005). Critical care: A color(full) analysis of care narratives in the schooling experiences of Puerto Rican girls. *American Educational Research Journal, 42*(1), 77–111.

Saltman, K. J. (2009). Corporatization and the control of schools. In M. W. Apple, W. Au, & L. A. Gandin (Eds.), *The Routledge international handbook of critical education* (pp. 54–63). New York, NY: Routledge.

Sarigianides, S. T., Lewis, M. A., & Petrone, R. (2015). How re-thinking adolescence helps re-imagine the teaching of English. *English Journal, 104*(3), 13–18.

Schargel, F., Thacker, T., & Bell, J. (2007). *From at-risk to academic excellence: What successful leaders do.* Larchmont, NY: Eye on Education.

Sealey-Ruiz, Y., & Greene, P. (2015). Popular visual images and the (mis) reading of Black male youth: A case for racial literacy in urban preservice teacher education. *Teaching Education, 26*(1), 55–76.

Sellers, R. M., & Shelton, J. N. (2003). The role of racial identity in perceived racial discrimination. *Journal of Personality and Social Psychology, 84,* 1070–1092.

Shulman, L. S. (1986). Those who understand: Knowledge and growth in teaching. *Educational Researcher, 15*(2), 4–14.

Shulman, L. S. (1987). Knowledge and teaching: Foundations of the new reform. *Harvard Educational Review, 57*(1), 1–23.

Sleeter, C. E. (2008). Teaching for democracy in an age of corporatocracy. *Teachers College Record, 110*(1), 139–159.

Sleeter, C. E., Neal, L. I., & Kumashiro, K. K. (2015). *Diversifying the teacher workforce: Preparing and retaining highly effective teachers.* New York, NY: Routledge.

Smagorinsky, P., Johnson, L. L., & Clayton, C. M. (2014). Synthesizing formal and experiential concepts in a service-learning course. In J. Brass & A. Webb (Eds.), *Reclaiming English language arts methods courses: Critical issues and challenges for teacher educators in top-down times* (pp. 123–134). New York, NY: Routledge.

Snyder, T. D., & Dillow, S. A. (2011). *Digest of Education Statistics 2010* (NCES 2011-015). U.S. Department of Education. Washington, DC: National Center for Education Statistics. Retrieved from nces.ed.gov/Pubsearch/Pubsinfo.Asp?Pubid=2011015

Soja, E. W. (1996). *Thirdspace: Journeys to Los Angeles and other real-and-imagined places.* Malden, MA: Blackwell.

Solórzano, D., Ceja, M., & Yosso, T. (2000, Winter). Critical race theory, racial microaggressions, and campus racial climate: The experiences of African American college students. *Journal of Negro Education, 69,* 60–73.

Stevenson, H. (2014). *Promoting racial literacy in schools: Differences that make a difference.* New York, NY: Teachers College Press.

Swaminathan, R. (2004). "It's my place": Student perspectives on urban school effectiveness. *School Effectiveness and School Improvement, 15*(1), 33–63.

Tuck, E. (2011). Humiliating ironies and dangerous dignities: A dialectic of school pushout. *International Journal of Qualitative Studies in Education, 24*(7), 817–827.

U2. (1993). Zooropa. On *Zooropa.* Dublin, Ireland: Island Records.

U.S. Department of Education. (2016, July). *The state of racial diversity in the educator workforce.* Retrieved from www2.ed.gov/rschstat/eval/highered/racial-diversity/state-racial-diversity-workforce.pdf

Van De Mieroop, D. (2015). Social identity theory and the discursive analysis of collective identities in narratives. In A. De Fina & A. Georgakopoulou (Eds.), *The handbook of narrative analysis* (pp. 408–428). Malden, MA: Wiley Blackwell.

Vasudevan, L., & Campano, G. (2009). The social production of adolescent risk and the promise of adolescent literacies. *Review of Research in Education, 33,* 310–353.

Vygotsky, L. S. (1978). *Mind in society: The development of higher psychological processes* (M. Cole, V. John-Steiner, S. Scribner & E. Souberman., Eds.) (A. R. Luria, M. Lopez-Morillas & M. Cole [with J. V. Wertsch], Trans.) Cambridge, MA: Harvard University Press. (Original manuscripts ca. 1930–1934).

Wald, J., & Losen, D. J. (2003). Defining and redirecting a school-to-prison pipeline. *New Directions for Youth Development, 99,* 9–15.

Ware, F. (2006). Warm demander pedagogy: Culturally responsive teaching that supports a culture of achievement for African American students. *Urban Education, 41*(4), 427–456.

Weis, L., & Fine, M. (Eds.). (2005). *Beyond silenced voices: Class, race, and gender in United States schools* (Rev. ed.). Albany, NY: State University of New York Press.

Wells, G. (1999). *Dialogic inquiry: Towards a sociocultural practice and theory of education.* Cambridge, UK: Cambridge University Press.

Wiles, J., & Bondi, J. (1980). *Supervision: A guide to practice.* Columbus, OH: Merrill.

Willis, A. I., Montavon, M., Hall, H., Hunger, C., Burke, L., & Herrera, A. (2008). *On critically conscious research: Approaches to language and literacy research.* New York, NY: Teachers College Press.

Willis, P. (1977). *Learning to labor: How working class kids get working class jobs*. New York, NY: Columbia University Press.

Wissman, K. (2007). "Making a way": Young women using literacy and language to resist the politics of silencing. *Journal of Adolescent and Adult Literacy, 51*(4), 340–349.

Wortham, S. (2001). *Narratives in action: A strategy for research and analysis*. New York, NY: Teachers College Press.

Wortham, S. (2004). From good student to outcast: The emergence of a classroom identity. *Ethos, 32*(2), 164–187.

Wortham, S.E.F. (1996). Mapping participant deictics: A technique for discovering speakers' footing. *Journal of Pragmatics, 25*, 331–348.

Index

About the Author

Deborah Bieler is an associate professor in the English education program at the University of Delaware. She is a former high school English teacher, student teaching mentor, and writing center director whose scholarship, teaching, and activism focus on the preparation and retention of equity-oriented secondary English teachers. Her work has appeared in journals such as *English Education*, *English Journal*, *Teachers College Record*, *Teacher Education Quarterly*, and *The New Educator*. She has received the National Council of Teachers of English Promising Researcher Award, the University of Delaware Trabant Award for Women's Equity, and the Conference on English Education Research Initiative Award.